The Invention of Ancient Slavery?

DUCKWORTH CLASSICAL ESSAYS

Series editor:
Thomas Harrison, University of Liverpool

Ancient Democracy and Modern Ideology
Peter Rhodes

Interpreting Classical Texts
Malcolm Heath

The Invention of Ancient Slavery
Niall McKeown

Reading Cicero:
Genre and Performance in Late Republican Rome
Catherine Steel

DUCKWORTH CLASSICAL ESSAYS

The Invention of Ancient Slavery?

Niall McKeown

Duckworth

First published in 2007 by
Gerald Duckworth & Co. Ltd.
90-93 Cowcross Street, London EC1M 6BF
Tel: 020 7490 7300
Fax: 020 7490 0080
inquiries@duckworth-publishers.co.uk
www.ducknet.co.uk

A catalogue record for this book is available
from the British Library

ISBN 978 07156 3185 0

Typeset by Ray Davies
Printed and bound in Great Britain by
MPG Books Ltd, Bodmin, Cornwall

Contents

Acknowledgements

Thanks most of all to those fine scholars whose work serves as the focus of my own. This book would not, however, exist without the assistance (and patience) of Deborah Blake at Duckworth. Or without Tom Harrison who commissioned it and helped enormously with editing.

Steve Hodkinson and Paul Cartledge, not directly involved with the book, gave crucial academic assistance on occasion. Thanks to all in the Institute of Archaeology and Antiquity in Birmingham, especially Mary Harlow, Gareth Sears and Gillian Shepherd, and also Vince Gaffney, Chris Wickham and Leslie Brubaker for reading grant applications. None are responsible for my errors or my arguments.

My thanks to my parents, John and Colette, and my wife Julia. Julia's theological background helped change my views of history writing. Lastly, my gratitude to all my teachers. They have included many of my students.

I would like to acknowledge gratefully the support of the Arts and Humanities Research Council in helping to fund the research leave enabling the completion of this book.

Introduction

A man, lost in the countryside, asks a farmer for directions. 'Ah sure,' says the farmer, 'I could tell you, but you don't want to be starting from here ...'

(Old Irish joke)

This is a book about some of the things historians want to believe about ancient slavery and how we manage to believe them. It is a book about the invention of the past, or rather of *a* past. It is about how the facts are given meaning. It is not, however, a book about conspiracy. It does not suggest that scholars are deliberately misrepresenting the facts. Rather it seeks to illustrate the compromises that *must* be made to produce an historical narrative. In examining the implications of those compromises it will raise the question how far any narrative of the past inevitably reflects our own values and what we want to find. Where we start from can indeed determine where we end up.

This is not a book about theory, but it is partly a reaction to a theoretical debate. Historians have always been concerned about difficulties in reconstructing the past. The last thirty years, however, have seen growing 'postmodern' criticism of traditional history writing. 'Postmodernists' have rejected the 'modernist' belief in a universe 'tamed' and made explicable. Instead they stress the difficulty of finding certainty, of achieving 'truth' and 'objectivity' (see, most famously, White 1978 and 1987, cf. Jenkins 1991 and 1995). They argue that historians have a double problem, as they are usually faced, paradoxically, with both too much information about the past and too little. Having more information about the past than they can fit into their narratives forces historians to edit, inevitably introducing a degree of subjectivity in deciding what to leave out. On the other hand, they never have the full facts about the past either, forcing them to use their imaginations to fill the gaps and provide a wider context for the material they do possess. The creation of any kind of narrative also involves a translation of past events into (our) words and concepts, allowing (potentially) a further drift in meaning. The criticism, at its most radical, is not just that different generations might ask different questions of the past, or apply different tools to understand it, but that key elements of our interpretation may reflect more what we want (or need) to believe than what actually happened (on this whole debate see e.g. Jenkins 1997; Fay and Pom 1998; Fox-Genovese 1999; Tosh 2000; Roberts 2001. Cf. Morley 1999: ch. 3).

This book is written in the shadow of the postmodern challenge. It focuses on the multiplicity of ways in which the story of the ancient slave has been, and is, written. At face value this multiplicity might suggest that there may be some truth in what postmodernists have had to say about historical 'truth'. I will certainly suggest they were right to raise issues about the notion of 'objectivity'. If I recognise the importance of their challenge, however, I am not necessarily a postmodernist. As Georg Iggers argued (2005: 119):

> There is ... a difference between a theory that denies any claim to reality in historical accounts and a historiography that is fully conscious of the complexity of historical knowledge but still assumes that real people had real thoughts and feelings that led to real actions that, within limits, can be known and reconstructed.

What are those limits with regard to ancient slavery? What are the 'rules' by which modern historians reconstruct the lives of slaves? How is the 'truth' arrived at? Some might argue that the ultimate judge of historical 'truth' is the community of professional scholars, and this has some merit. Whatever the divide between, for example, a Russian Marxist historian (Chapter 3) or a German conservative historian (Chapter 2), each would be mortified if, for example, it were discovered that they had simply invented parts of their evidence. This would be outside the 'rules of the game' for both. Unfortunately, scholars, as we will show in detail throughout this book, have excellent ways of dealing with difficult data *within the rules*. We might hope that 'history' will produce a single, comprehensible, authoritative viewpoint, but the reality can be very different. The evidence, as we shall see, can be used to draw very different pictures.

This book will look at a sample of some of the very best historians of ancient slavery, particularly Roman slavery. It examines how they have produced their interpretations. It is not, therefore, a potted history of ancient slavery, or, indeed, of the historians who have written that history. We shall see that, however rigorous and logical historians might be, there remain gaps in their narratives. We shall examine how they fill those gaps. Just as in traditional cinema the illusion of movement is given by many different still pictures, so historians use a professional sleight of hand to produce a narrative usable to their readers. It is time to explore this, the true 'magic' of ancient history.

1

The Changing Face of Roman Slavery

At any one time in the period between 200 BC and AD 200 between 5 and 10% of the 50-100 million inhabitants of the Roman empire may have been slaves. It is often said that they left behind little evidence. This is true in the sense that they produced little literature and authors from the Roman elite were generally unconcerned with slaves. On the other hand, hundreds of thousands of inscriptions (often tombstones) have survived from the Roman empire. Some tens of thousands of these mention slaves, particularly freed slaves. However short the majority of these inscriptions might be, they still represent a formidable corpus of evidence. I want here to examine some of the ways historians have used this material. They highlight some of the fundamental problems with the way we tell stories about the past. In order, ultimately, to throw light on the mental boxes within which *we* currently operate, I will attempt to show a few of the 'mental boxes' within which earlier writers have constructed their interpretations.

Let us go back in time some seventy years and imagine that we were reading about ancient slavery some time in the 1930s, in Britain or the USA. Many different stories could be told of Roman slavery, but let us examine just one that was prominent then.

First, a little context. The major literary texts on Roman history (e.g. the histories of Livy or the biographies of Suetonius) had been widely read for centuries. In the nineteenth and early twentieth centuries, however, the systematic examination of epitaphs and other inscriptions was given increasing emphasis. In 1916 Tenney Frank published a statistical analysis of over 10,000 inscriptions from Roman Italy. He argued that the vast majority of epitaphs, particularly from Rome, were of freed slaves, apparently coming from the eastern, Greek, half of the Mediterranean. This was particularly noteworthy since slaves of Roman citizens (unlike, for example, their counterparts in the USA in the nineteenth century) usually became citizens themselves when they were freed. Frank suggested that perhaps 90% of the population of the city of Rome 'had Oriental blood in their veins' – mainly from (freed) slaves (Frank 1916: 690). Rome, indeed all of urban Italy, was a 'melting pot' (703). Frank felt his conclusions were supported by contemporary Roman literary sources. The historian Tacitus and the satirist Juvenal both complained that the poor (and even the aristocracy) of the city of Rome were increasingly marked by servile descent (689). The picture was reinforced when Mary Gordon, in a separate epigraphic analysis in 1931, found that more than 20% of those holding municipal office in Italy during the 'Golden Age' of Rome (roughly the second century AD) apparently came from freedman, ex-slave, families (Gordon 1931: 70).

Our 1930s reader would quickly have discovered a number

of recurrent themes in the way in which English-speaking historians typically reacted to this material. I will concentrate here on some of the work of Frank and Gordon and on the 1928 monographs by Barrow and Duff devoted to Roman slaves and freedmen.

(1) Historians were well aware that the elite Roman authors whose work had survived were often contemptuous of outsiders and those who could not support themselves independently from their landed estates. Many slaves were foreign (though see Chapter 6), and many freed slaves were skilled labourers, dependent for their living upon their customers. The contempt for ex-slaves is most famously captured in the depiction of Trimalchio, a fabulously rich freedman who appears in Petronius' comic novel *The Satyricon*. His education and taste never match his fabulous wealth: we first meet him while he is urinating publicly (*Satyricon* 27). The contempt is also seen in Tacitus' venomous portrayal in his *Annals* of the slaves and freedmen who staffed much of the emperor's administration. One could compare finally the bile directed at fawning good-for-nothing (but successful) easterners in Juvenal's splenetic third *Satire*.

(2) It was recognised that there were potential difficulties with such portraits (e.g. Frank 1916: 705). How 'realistic' were they, or how far were they a product of jealousy directed against 'outsiders' who had made good? Was it safe to accept the picture given by comedic genres such as satire? Was there a danger of unthinkingly reproducing the racism and snobbery of elite Romans? Many slaves and freedmen, modern writers recognised, made important contributions to Roman society,

and the complaints of Juvenal, Tacitus and others were doubtless exaggerated (Barrow 1928: 198, 206-7; Duff 1928: 97).

(3) It was felt, however, that there was 'no smoke without fire'. Bringing slaves into the body politic was allegedly a bad idea, for two reasons. First, racial mixture, particularly involving easterners, could only serve to dilute the energy of the Roman people. Frank described it as 'race suicide' (1916: 704). Second, even for those who, like Gordon, might have some doubts about unthinking references to 'racial characteristics' (1931: 76-7), the degrading life slaves had led before being freed could only have undermined their moral fibre (77). It all led, according to Barrow (1928: 26), to a situation in which

the Syrian profligate stood by as a tempter to whisper the promise of new vice in the ear of the descendant of a Roman family once famous for hardness and simplicity, but now too enervated to resist.

And Tenney Frank (1916: 705) argued that

This Orientalizing of Rome's populace has a more important bearing than is usually accorded it upon the larger question of why the spirit and acts of imperial Rome are totally different from those of the republic, if indeed racial characteristics are not wholly a myth. There is today a healthy activity in the study of the economic factors ... that contributed to Rome's decline. But what lay behind and constantly reacted upon all such causes of Rome's disintegration was, after all, to a considerable extent, the fact that the people who built Rome had given way to a different race. The lack of energy and enterprise, the failure of foresight and common sense, the weakening of moral and political stamina, all were concomitant with the gradual diminution of the stock which, during the earlier days, had displayed these qualities.

(4) As that quotation illustrates, however, historians such as Frank clearly recognised that there were problems with this theory, not least that there were also other possible ways of explaining Roman decline (for the most recent discussion, see Ward-Perkins 2005). Frank and others were ready, however, to deal with evidence and cases which apparently flew in the face of their theories. For example, some of the aristocrats of the good Roman stock Frank so admired had behaved rather badly during the time of the early emperors (1916: 706):

... when, on reading Tacitus, we are amazed at the new servility of Scipios and Messalas [grand old aristocratic families], we must recall that these scattered inheritors of the old aristocratic ideals had at their back only an alien rabble of ex-slaves, to whom they would have appealed in vain for a return to ancestral ideas of law and order. They had little choice between servility and suicide, and not a few chose the latter.

If easterners were so decadent, how had they managed to

create what appeared to be a very successful and long-lived urban civilisation for themselves? (Barrow 1928: 218):

> In Asia Minor and Syria the intermingling of Greek and Oriental blood and culture had gone on for centuries; the result was an urban life marvellous for its outward splendour. Yet those who knew it best knew the decadence within.

There was another problem. If 'Orientals' or descendants of slaves had created the decay, why did the Roman empire continue for centuries after the peak of their influx? Barrow suggested that Oriental vices might lie dormant for a while, not least because they lacked the 'vitality to express themselves'. As east mingled with west those vices were, however, gradually given impetus by western 'vigour'. Everything might appear normal for a while but 'inherited dispositions' would eventually, inevitably, reassert themselves (Barrow 1928: 216-17):

> Heredity, climate, institutions have always proved fatal to the Western race rash enough to ally itself too closely with the East.

Finally, if some societies were able to benefit from racial mixture, that was obviously because they had the correct mixture of races (Duff 1928: 206):

> The question whether foreign blood benefits a nation or not cannot yet be answered dogmatically. The Anglo-

Saxon race has not suffered from its Celtic, Danish and Norman elements, to say nothing of Flemish and Huguenot immigrants. On the other hand race-mixture hastened the decline of the Persian Empire, and American statesmen to-day are justifiably alarmed by alien immigration.

(5) As Duff's comments illustrate, historians often had a modern analogy to hand to illuminate their theories, and their analogies imply that their view of modern immigration and race mixture might have been as negative as their view of its impact upon Rome. Here, for example, is Frank (1916: 707-8):

One after another the emperors gained popularity with the rabble by erecting a shrine to some foreign Baal, or a statue to Isis in his chapel, in much the same way that our cities are lining their park drives with tributes to Garibaldi, Pulaski, and who knows what –vitch.

Duff was to argue that manumission was not a problem in the USA *until after the Civil War* (1928: 1). Gordon, when examining the honours given to rich freedmen and recorded in inscriptions, found herself 'unpleasantly reminded of the accusations sometimes brought against the recipients of "birthday honours" ' (1931: 74).

There were some historians who dissented from the picture outlined above, such as Dill and Rostovtzeff, but their work also suggests how difficult it was to divorce modern politics from ancient history. Dill, ignoring the ridicule of prejudiced

Romans (1904: 101-2), saw manumission as a boon to Roman society, bringing about a 'vigorous mercantile class'. In a manner which might remind readers of the changes in British society in the Victorian era, he argued that rich freedmen were 'becoming great capitalists and landowners on a senatorial stage' (100). The Russian emigré Michael Rostovtzeff in his *Social and Economic History of the Roman Empire*, originally published in 1926, saw 'no criterion for distinguishing between inferior and superior races' (1926: 485). The lesson he learned from the decline of the empire, however, perhaps had some echoes of events in his homeland after the revolution (486):

> ... violent attempts at levelling have never helped to uplift the masses. They have destroyed the upper classes, and resulted in accelerating the process of barbarization. But the ultimate problem remains like a ghost, ever present and unlaid: Is it possible to extend a higher civilization to the lower classes without debasing its standard and diluting its quality to the vanishing point? Is not every civilization bound to decay as soon as it starts to penetrate the masses?

The views of Frank, Barrow and Duff would probably have appeared very much the orthodoxy to an undergraduate of the 1930s, however. Indeed, astonishingly, much of their work remains important today. Barrow's book was the only English textbook on its topic until Keith Bradley's *Slaves and Masters in the Roman Empire* in 1984 (indeed, there is a 1996 reprint). Even more remarkably, Duff's work *remains* the only textbook on freedmen in the imperial period. For the purpose of student bibliographies they obviously remain classics: texts that everyone mentions but that no one (particularly the tutors putting them on their reading lists) actually reads.

The crucial point about historians such as Frank, Duff and Barrow is that they clearly had (Roman) evidence on which to base their opinions, and their views were consistent with that material. Given the way that Romans looked at non-Romans (see e.g. Sherwin-White 1967; Balsdon 1979; Isaac 2004), racist views of Roman history were never going to lack for evidence. Frank and the rest recognised problems with their theories but believed they had dealt with them. They were writing proper history. I do not wish to be misunderstood. I am not seeking to argue (alongside some Aryan US websites!) that the racial/ servile 'explanation' of Rome's decline is correct. The nature of the evidence, however, certainly allowed Barrow and the others to argue this case. It also makes it oddly difficult to disprove them, even if it is comparatively easy to suggest possible *doubts*.

What position might a student have adopted in the 1930s, and why? One might like to believe that the side with better arguments or more evidence would prevail. But the arguments on each side (e.g. Dill versus Duff) cannot easily be compared with one another from internal criteria alone, leaving our student to make her final choice as we might choose a newspaper, looking for the editorial voice which most closely reflects our own core values. Let us now jump forward 60 years and examine how a student of the 1990s might have approached the issue of Roman freedmen. Luckily we had by then become much cleverer and better historians, with a greater capacity to avoid the pitfalls of reading our society into the past. Or had we?

In 1969 Susan Treggiari published a survey of Roman freedmen during the late Republic. She distanced herself clearly from Frank's position (1969: 238):

> Since Tenney Frank wrote his article on race mixture in 1916, the whole theory of racial purity has been discredited and it would hardly be suggested any longer that if freedmen originated in the eastern half of the empire they necessarily possessed determinable racial characteristics which would, by a sort of chemical formula, spoil the virtues of the Roman people.

She is, of course, correct. Such views *are* no longer acceptable, though it is interesting that she was prepared to argue that the 'racial mixture would certainly dilute the Roman character' but that slaves would have been rendered less alien partly because 'the new citizens served a period of probation in Roman households' (237). Overall, Treggiari offers a generally very positive view of the contribution of Roman ex-slaves to Republican Rome (240):

> many brought the idealism of Greece to the ancient Roman pragmatism. If we read [the poet] Horace's account of his father the freedman we feel that it is full of what we should be inclined to regard as typically Roman virtues: common sense, a strict moral code, dislike of sham and ostentation. Freedmen were not necessarily out of tune with their Roman environment. Often they

both absorbed much that was good in native life and contributed to Rome their own culture and values.

There were some disreputable ex-slaves but there was nothing to suggest their characters would have been different had they been born free (241).

The views of Duff and Barrow have been turned on their heads. Whom should we believe, and why? Andrew Wallace-Hadrill's 1994 book, *Houses and Society in Pompeii and Herculaneum*, investigated links between Roman architecture and social history. He criticised some earlier Italian scholarship which suggested a 'decline' in the domestic architecture and art of Pompeii connected with a new 'vulgar' freedman immigrant population (1994: ch. 6). Wallace-Hadrill elegantly pointed out the many inconsistencies and unexamined premises of such arguments, e.g. the tendency simply to assume that poor taste was symptomatic of the freedman and the trader. Using a cache of legal documents found in Herculaneum involving a freedman called Venidius Ennychus, he sought to give a very different picture of Roman society (ch. 8). Where others had seen dangers to racial purity, he saw something different (183):

The defeat of fascism, and the longer battle against racism, have transformed the ideologies through which we approach and interrogate the past. In a postimperialist world troubled by the problems of ethnicity and integration of immigrant populations, we may still turn to the Roman world for a success story, not this time of conquest and enslavement but of coping with the unexpected consequences. Venidius Ennychus in his handsome black salon, looking so much as if he *belongs*, becomes a symbol not of the collapse of a respectable Italian town but of the success of a new social system. From our own vantage point, we can appreciate that social integration is achieved through cultural transformation.

I am fairly confident which of the two main interpretations of Roman freedmen (the unease of the early twentieth or the celebration of the late twentieth century) most of my readers are likely to share. I prefer the latter too. That, however, may have little to do with the actual evidence. Let me illustrate why. Time travel is one of the great pleasures allowed the historian. Bringing the dead back to life is another. If Frank and Barrow and Duff could be revived and confronted by Treggiari or Wallace-Hadrill, how likely is it that they would be convinced by them? Let us assume (for we have no reason to assume otherwise) that they were honest people whose intelligence was at least equal to our own. I suspect they would have seen little reason to shift their positions. They might accept, for reasons we shall see shortly, that some of their estimates of the number of 'easterners' in the population of Rome were probably too high, but this may not of itself have lessened their fears of the effect of slavery upon individuals or society. They had always accepted that authors such as Tacitus and Juvenal were biased against freedmen, but believed, nonetheless, they their criticisms contained an element of truth. They probably would have felt no reason to put greater trust instead in Horace's praise of the virtues of his freedman father, even though they accepted that *some* ex-slaves had made an important contribution to Roman society. Barrow and Duff would have argued that the very fact that Venidius Ennychus looked as if he 'belonged' in Herculaneum, and the social changes that Wallace-Hadrill celebrates, were, for many Roman writers, precisely the problem. Wallace-Hadrill might feel that his story of Venidius Ennychus' 'success' in Herculaneum was a worthwhile interpretation of the past for 'a postimperialist world troubled by the problems of ethnicity and integration of immigrant populations', but Barrow would no doubt have felt his interpretation was worthwhile for an imperialist world troubled by exactly the same things. Barrow and Duff felt that their position was backed by a mass of ancient evidence. More recent authors have chosen to portray that evidence as mere snobbery and exaggeration. They may very well be correct. But how can they prove it? And if they can't prove it, how could they hope to convince someone like Tenney Frank? Generally, rather than reply to earlier interpretations, more recent historians have simply chosen (as we shall see) to stress different things.

I am in no way attempting to 'prove' or support a racist view of history (which, quite frankly, I find morally repugnant), but to investigate what happened to this particular racist paradigm. In effect it simply disappeared. It was ignored rather than rebutted, partly because, in its own terms, rebuttal was very difficult. We have apparently just moved on. That may be a very good thing, but it is a good thing with little necessarily to do with the nature of our evidence from the past. While modern scholars dealing with evidence of Roman slavery from inscriptions have largely left behind them insoluble questions about race, they have moved on, as we shall see, to some equally insoluble questions that better reflect the politics of our own day.

By the middle part of the last century serious doubts were being raised about the uses made by Frank and others of the epigraphic evidence. Epitaphs would have been costly and provide us only with a tiny sample of those who lived and died. Suspiciously, the age at death and sex of those we meet in inscriptions are almost certainly not a representative sample of the whole population (as noted by Keith Hopkins in 1966). Lily Ross Taylor argued in 1961 that the enormous proportion of the freedmen among the commemorated was also unlikely to be representative of the overall population, since it implied that they virtually never had any children. Those children ought to appear as free people in epitaph statistics, but do not. Large sections of the free population seem not to have left behind an epitaph we can read today. For these reasons (and others), it may be dangerous to estimate the proportions of different 'races' in Rome from surviving inscriptions. This might perhaps have affected the views of Frank or Duff or Barrow on the negative impact of race and slavery (depending, of course, on how low a proportion of slaves or easterners they felt was sufficient to 'corrupt' society).

The 'over-representation' of freedmen in extant inscriptions is now generally accepted as proven (see e.g. Saller 2001: 109). Why this happened is much less clear. A number of different theories have been put forward, sometimes in combination. Ex-slaves may have been particularly keen to leave a marker showing that they had moved up in the world. Grave markers are also important ways of showing family connections. In Roman law slaves had no family. Perhaps ex-slaves who could create secure families wanted especially to memorialise this (e.g. Taylor 1961; Mouritsen 2004, 2005; Zanker 1975). Some historians have pointed out, however, that (a) slaves were far from the only group to leave behind inscriptions (the very wealthy and many free people living in the provinces did it too) and (b) the widespread use of inscriptions comes largely from a specific period of time: the first three centuries AD). They therefore search for a wider explanation of the phenomenon (e.g. Meyer 1990; Woolf 1996). The early empire was a time of massive social change. Perhaps inscriptions were a way not only for those who were rising in the world to express their new status by writing it in stone, but also for those who feared falling in society to try to fix their current status by doing the same. Slaves may have caught the so-called 'epigraphic habit' initially from their social betters (who may then have started to abandon the practice as it lost its social exclusivity). Perhaps all those who managed to gain Roman citizenship (be they ex-slaves or provincials) wanted to show off their new status (eventually granted to all freeborn within the empire in AD 212, so losing its special significance, and potentially explaining the decline in the number of inscriptions in the third century). It is difficult if not impossible to choose between some of these interpretations, but which you choose has very different implications for our picture of Roman freedmen (did they, as the first theory suggested, value their families more than free-born Romans, or not?). The precise purpose of memorialisation still remains unclear, which makes Sandra Joshel's contribution to the debate all the more interesting. Her 1992 book, *Work, Identity and Legal Status at Rome* also illustrates once more how different our readings of this material are compared to those of seventy years ago. It also introduces a subject that will become a common theme in this book: slave resistance.

Joshel tackled a fundamental problem: how do we reconstruct the past when almost all our evidence is generated by a particular group (elite Romans) with its own agenda. Traditional rules for establishing the truth from our evidence (e.g. its internal consistency) fail to help us much because of the biases built into the original material (e.g. the racism and snobbery of those elite Romans). We have a partial view (in every sense of the word), leaving us in danger of accepting the silencing of particular groups (be they women, or slaves, or the poor) (1992: 13):

> However 'true,' historical accounts based on these sources must be viewed as fictions and as partial. Yet, if we attempt to fill the gap by reading the epitaphs of Roman workers and tradesmen with assumptions drawn from legal and literary texts, we simply reinscribe hegemony and exclusion, and we are led, conceptually, by the viewpoint of the master.

She showed that comparison with slave societies where we have more direct testimony (e.g. the USA in the nineteenth century), has shown that literary stereotypes can (often purposely) hide the truth rather than help to reveal it.

1. The Changing Face of Roman Slavery

Determined not just to repeat the bias of aristocratic Roman authors such as Petronius, Joshel examined epitaphs from Rome where the trade of the dead person was mentioned. Slaves and freedmen, particularly the former, seemed unusually keen to have their occupation mentioned on inscriptions, which would appear to contradict the contempt of the elite for those who worked for a living. Joshel suggested that the slaves/ freedmen were stressing their social worth and a community with other slaves and freedmen. This claim to activity also threw into pointed relief the *in*activity of the slaveowner/ patron. Society might try to deny slaves their identity: *they* insisted upon it. This is a cheering story, but there is a problem. Joshel admits that the Roman elite themselves often identified their servants by their jobs. This makes the 'opposition' to the master seen on the inscriptions particularly subtle, since the elite would not necessarily have read it as resistance at all (160):

> Ironically ... the use of work to frame an identity would not have been viewed by the slaveholder as dangerous and rebellious.

This leads us to question whether what was being expressed was not resistance, but an *acceptance* of the norms given by the masters, as some earlier authors discussed by Joshel had suggested.

Joshel's aim of recovering the slave from the silence imposed by the masters is a noble one. Certainly, she has enriched the range of possible and plausible readings of this material. She was fully aware of the provisional nature of her readings (see e.g. ch. 1 and p. 163). Her results are appealing (certainly to me) and very possibly correct (as her use of US material might suggest). But they *could* be wrong, and what is the basis on which we might choose this *potential* interpretation of the evidence over another? Because it is appealing? We can be too keen to create a narrative from the scattered evidence from the past when that evidence can actually support a number of narratives. Crucially, proving that the position of previous scholars (which implied a more socially conformist attitude among slaves) *may* be wrong or that its evidence is ambiguous is not equivalent to proving its opposite (that these inscriptions illustrate slave resistance). Posing an alternative view is not equivalent to showing that it is a better alternative, as sometimes seems to be implied.

I am not claiming we can say nothing about slavery through reading inscriptions. There has been a series of fundamental works using epigraphy to examine (e.g.) the emperor's freedmen (Weaver 1972; Chantraine 1967; Boulvert 1970), slaves belonging to cities (Weiß 2004), and the organisation of Roman industries (Prachner 1980). One cannot doubt the evidence of the political impact of freed families on Roman towns (Garnsey 1975, 1981). I am, admittedly, rather less sure whether we can establish sensible estimates from the epigraphic record of the likely rates at which slaves were freed (compare Alföldy 1972 with Wiedemann 1985). It needs to be stressed, however, that none of the historians cited in this chapter is a bad historian: indeed, they are among the finest. They illustrate, however, some of the potential pitfalls in interpretation that we must be aware of. They also illustrate, today just as much in the 1930s, the fact that the way we choose to interpret ancient slavery has much to do with the way we want to interpret it. The problem is not so much that we invent the past as that, when we explore it, we tend to find what we are looking for. Often, when we appear to claim that 'this is the way it actually was', we are, in practice, asking the reader to share our ethical ideals, which is something very different. In the following chapters we shall examine what that implies, and how different authors deal in contrasting ways with the surviving evidence about ancient slavery.

2

Ancient Slavery and Modern Geography

In the last chapter I showed some of the ways in which our view of Roman slavery has changed over time and why those dramatic changes have been possible. In the following chapters I want to give just a taste of the very different ways historians have tackled this subject recently and the implications of these different approaches for our understanding of the lives of slaves. I will concentrate on a number of individual examples so that we can examine the detail of their work.

Every cloud has a silver lining: Fridolf Kudlien and the slave in Roman oracles

More than three dozen books have been published since 1950 as part of the Mainz Academy's project, *Forschungen zur antiken Sklaverei* (Researches on Ancient Slavery). They represent perhaps the single biggest research project on the topic. Despite this, they are virtually unknown to British students, firstly because they were written in German and have not been translated; secondly because their work was greeted with suspicion in some parts of the Anglophone academic world. While I was a graduate student in the 1980s the clear implication was conveyed to me that they were books best avoided, somehow a product of dubious post-war German right-wing politics (see Finley 1998: ch. 1 esp. 123ff.). This was a prejudice I was happy to pass on to my own students. That was until I actually finally read the *Forschungen* and the work associated with them. What I found was often subtly, sometimes strikingly, different from what I had expected. The 'Mainz' material posed a real challenge to my academic world-view. It was not that I necessarily agreed with authors such as Vogt or Lauffer or Kudlien, but I found them much more difficult to rebut than I had expected (and hoped). I discovered that the unexamined assumptions they sometimes shared (and which I dutifully attacked) often simply formed a reverse image to the unexamined assumptions of my own 'liberal Anglophone' approach. The shock of this realisation was a key element in the genesis of this book.

The *Forschungen* were interesting and provocative for a number of reasons. Many engaged polemically with both Anglophone (British and US) and particularly eastern European (Marxist) orthodoxies. They wanted to challenge the view that slaves were seen by Roman society simply as property to exploit. They often denied that slaves had any significant group ('class') consciousness. They tended to emphasise types of evidence (for example, inscriptions) that had not always been well mined by other historians of slavery (despite what we saw in the last chapter). Finally they wanted to understand how slavery survived as long as it did. Some of the *Forschungen* might therefore be described as broadly 'functionalist' in approach, looking more at how the slave system kept operating than at the strains that might have pulled it apart. It should be stressed, however, that the Mainz project was far from monolithic. Some of the monographs were largely technical examinations of particular institutions or sets of evidence. More recently the project has begun to focus on legal texts which may lead to a greater stress on conflict and exploitation (see Gamaulf 2001, though compare Waldstein 1986, 2001). Even in the earlier years of the project the monographs of Hans Klees (1975 and especially 1998) showed that individual authors could produce work whose emphasis on exploitation and conflict was very close to orthodox positions within the English-speaking world. I want to look closely at Fridolf Kudlien's 1991 book on the evidence on ancient slavery in responses given to individuals by oracles, not because the book is somehow 'typical' of the Mainz *Forschungen* ('typical' is probably not a very useful idea in this context), but because it illustrates some the most striking differences from much Anglophone scholarship.

Kudlien, like many other Mainz authors, examined a body of material (including astrological handbooks and dream interpretations) not often used by other historians of slavery. These texts survive, however, in surprisingly large numbers (particularly from the mid- to later Roman empire), and make frequent reference to slaves. Astonishingly the oracles occasionally even gave slaves advice on issues such as running away (e.g. 118, 127, from the *Sortes Astrampsychi* and *Sortes Sangallenses*). Further, precisely because they lack literary merit (and so are not likely to be the creation of the elite), Kudlien argued that they are more likely to connect us with the lives of ordinary people (esp. 20-8). He recognised that some slaves living isolated existences (e.g. miners) might be underrepresented in these texts (24-5) but felt that this did not undermine their importance.

Kudlien argued that one should not use isolated reports to exaggerate either the loyalty of, or cruelty towards, slaves (14). Further, rather than look at just social control of slaves (as many Anglophone historians have done), he was more interested in the more human aspects of the slave's existence: their hopes and fears, loves and aspirations (10). He criticised what he saw as the lazy and one-sided interpretation of ancient slavery that argued slaves were 'socially dead'. This emphasised the rightlessness of slaves and the hopelessness of slave life too much (e.g. 12-14, 150-4). There were, of course, clear negative aspects of ancient slavery, for example the mutual fear of violence between master and slave (see e.g. 45, 49-53, 78, 109-10). The 'social death' position was, nevertheless, too one-sided. It simply reproduced, he argued, the anti-slave snobbery of a few ancient writers who viewed slaves as non-human and as (tame) animals (153). Some authors were thinking too much of the Nazi concentration camps when they wrote about ancient slavery, particularly (he felt) some Jewish scholars (ibid.). He argued that such a 'concentration camp' view underestimated the capacity of slaves to make their own world. Slaves were not just things. It might have been ill-judged (indeed wrong) for Joseph Vogt, one-time editor of the Mainz *Forschungen*, to write about the connections between ancient slavery and 'humanity' (156): slavery by its nature was an inhumane institution. Humans still affected that institution, however, with human emotions of both master and slave complicating affairs (e.g. 157).

Kudlien admitted that there was an 'unpleasant' side to slavery. This included mistrust and fear between master and slave, the contempt in which slaves were often held, and even sadistic physical and sexual abuse (151). There was, however, something else, which Kudlien described as the 'pleasant' side: affection and loyalty between master and slave (157-8). For example, while the reality of sexual abuse should 'in no way be disputed or toned down' this gave only one side of a complex problem (40). He cited examples where sexual relations between master and slave do appear to lead to real affection (42, quoting Keith Bradley, the stress of whose work was, paradoxically, usually the opposite to Kudlien's):

> [On the other hand] there was for slaves, without doubt ... the possibility of 'relationships with their owners which were founded on genuine sentiment', that means relationships in which slaves did not have to play the role of involuntary lovers ...

One might question the particulars of some of Kudlien's evidence, but overall he has a point. There were doubtless *some* occasions where sexual relations between master (or even mistress) and slave entailed real emotional ties. Similarly, although oracles might indicate that a slave could be frightened of being sold to a new home, there was also another side: the (happy) anticipation in oracles of being sold to a *wealthier* home, perhaps even that of the emperor (89-90 and 78, citing Artemidorus, *The Interpretation of Dreams*

2.68). For Kudlien (and, he believed, Roman slaves) many clouds had a silver lining.

Kudlien does admit that fear of punishment appears to be quite common but argues that this was only one 'aspect of slave mentality'. Its importance would have been determined by the temperament of individual masters (45-6):

> We have seen that true, positive, deep-reaching relations of intimacy were possible between the two unequal partners, relations that could ameliorate the situation of fear typical of slaves, if they couldn't make it disappear. And, among the many individual cases, as happened besides time and time again in the nature of things, there was also the opposite: a dependence, amounting even to a certain fear, of a master on a specific, very valued slave.

The oracles, argued Kudlien, allow us to see some of the hopes of slaves as well as their fears. Some of the texts speak of loyalty and even love between master and slave as well as between slaves (see, e.g. 38ff.). They suggested a largely 'conformist' attitude among slaves (159-60). The idea that slaves were interested only in flight or in freedom was, he claimed, exaggerated. Slaves wonder if they will gain promotion, including adoption into their master's household (e.g. 120-2). Romans often called their slaves *'puer'* – 'boy'. Kudlien suggested that this did not necessarily 'dehumanise' the slave but could be neutral, even positive. It might, he argued, express belonging within a household, in the same manner as a child (39-40). Much of what slaves hoped for (health, occasionally a family) was common to slave and free, reminiscent of the attitudes of the 'petty bourgeois', or the conservatism of modern industrial workers (155).

> The existence of a 'pleasant side of slavery' represents here not the exception, but continually real possibilities which were again and again realisable and realised (152).

> That domestic slaves in antiquity were [recognised as] 'persons' in principle, actual human individuals with a sometimes even quite pronounced mentality, can and should no longer be sensibly denied. Look at this mentality as a whole. One notices a wholly dominating tendency towards a system-maintaining and stabilising conformity among domestic slaves. There was, however often insubordination towards masters or flight in individual cases (154).

On some important levels, Kudlien is almost certainly correct (at least in the terms in which he has engaged in the debate). This may seem shocking to writers educated in an Anglophone tradition, but that is at least partly because we have been conditioned to react badly to such arguments, irrespective of their merits. Concentration camp analogies do fit ill with the groups of urban and domestic slaves he focuses upon (though, significantly, not necessarily slaves on farms or in mines). In addition, his evidence does indicate some affective relationships between masters and slaves. Any history that ignores (or even marginalises) such relationships is inevitably (and usually deliberately) giving a one-sided picture of ancient slavery, and particularly urban slavery.

2. Ancient Slavery and Modern Geography

There are also, however, clear difficulties with Kudlien's picture. It is all very well picking an extreme opponent and showing that his position is exaggerated, but concentration camp analogies have usually been asides: they hardly reflect the complexity with which Finley or any other serious scholar viewed the whole institution. Undermining such an exaggeration might *imply* its opposite (a relatively harmonious relationship between master and slave: certainly the impression many readers would have on finishing Kudlien's book), but it does not prove it. Masters may not have treated their slaves simply as animals, but what does that tell us about the affective relations Kudlien is keen to sketch? Does it mean that they were universal/ typical/ common/ *merely possible*? What are the implications of one's choice, and how does one make it? There is little to guide the reader of Kudlien's book (though we shall see that this affects most other writers on the subject too).

The problem can be seen, for example, in Kudlien's treatment of the sexual abuse of slaves. His argument takes the form 'one shouldn't underestimate the sexual abuse by masters of their slaves, *but* ...'. One could legitimately wonder, however, quite how important it was that *some* slaves who slept with their masters may have felt strong bonds to them. What of the others? Where might we expect to hear the voices of those who *didn't* enjoy the experience? Similarly, how far should we stress the importance of the psychology of the individual, given a system which put slaves in a position where they could be so easily abused? Kudlien was indulging (quite deliberately) in polemic, putting a side of the story which he felt was sometimes repressed (one of the strengths of much of the Mainz *Forschungen* from an Anglophone perspective). That, however, can be very different from giving an account of what *typically* happened.

The same is true also of Kudlien's insistence on the 'petty bourgeois' nature of slave thinking he sees in the responses to oracles. This, if true, would certainly help to undermine any idea of ancient slaves being a 'revolutionary proletariat' (long a bugbear of the Mainz *Forschungen* and long in retreat, even in eastern Europe, before Kudlien's book was published). Kudlien showed that slaves did not *just* wish for freedom but could have the same hopes and fears as free people in these texts, but it is less clear what this implies. One would hardly expect slaves *only* to have had dreams about freedom, and even Kudlien admits that they seem to have had plenty of those (e.g. 80 and 83). Slaves were (as even ancient slaveowners admitted) human beings, and it should be little surprise that they shared human hopes and fears. This does not mean they had exactly the same hopes and fears as the free. Kudlien may be rescuing the 'more pleasant' side of slavery from what he regards as unmerited oblivion, but it is clear even from his own text that the 'unpleasant' side was still very important. Free people may worry about promotion, or even hope for adoption, they are less likely to worry about being beaten by a master, or plan flight, or dream of freedom (see above).

The overall emphasis given by Kudlien's text can therefore seem a little arbitrary. Kudlien may parade a handful of examples of slaves hoping to be adopted by their master (84, 121, 126). There are (as Kudlien would accept) far, far more references (for example) to possible flight by slaves. Clearly the *possibility* of adoption did exist, but it seems a fairly minor element in the psychologies revealed by Kudlien's corpus of evidence. One might emphasise it precisely because it is surprising, but what does that tell us about the world of even (relatively privileged) domestic slaves?

Sometimes Kudlien (in common, as we shall see, with all other historians) had to try hard to explain away evidence. We have noted above a striking number of references to potential conflicts between slave and free in Kudlien's oracular texts. Whether or not they reflected 'revolutionary' movements seeking to overthrow slavery, they nonetheless apparently illustrate tensions between masters and slaves. Kudlien tried to make the evidence go away by suggesting that in modern Germany there was often considerable paranoia about an imaginary 'threat' from Jews, even when none existed (51). This may be quite true, but this kind of analogy does not constitute any form of proof in itself. It represents a *possible* way of rejecting the evidence for conflict between slave and owner, but its plausibility is linked to the persuasiveness of Kudlien's overall theory about the harmoniousness of slave/ master relations. Again, he has certainly produced an alternative, but hasn't shown how and why his alternative is better.

If one can have legitimate differences of interpretation over the oracular texts that Kudlien cited, there are also, interestingly, texts that he didn't cite. As we mentioned earlier, historians generally cannot discuss everything in their field: they have to edit. Kudlien noted that the fear of being enslaved appears in these texts but did not fully deal with its implication (46-9). He mentioned a fear of 'loss of security', but surely the fear of enslavement in our evidence represents something rather more drastic than that. It is interesting that some of the texts of the dream interpreter Artemidorus that he *fails* to cite actually suggest that slavery was clearly seen as drudgery, whereas mastership is having the power to do what one wants with someone (see e.g. *The Interpretation of Dreams* 2.27, 3.18, 3.28). It is symptomatic that Keith Bradley used Artemidorus to stress precisely how *miserable* the life of the slave could be (1994: 140-5). Such texts, of course, don't negate the 'more pleasant' aspects of slavery Kudlien suggested elsewhere, but they may imply that such 'pleasant' aspects were not necessarily those that came to mind immediately when Artemidorus and other writers within the Roman empire thought about the institution.

Despite these criticisms, there are, as already noted, several important areas in which Kudlien was almost certainly correct. Some of his attacks did hit home. For example, the assumption that the use of '*puer*' or 'boy' to denote a slave *necessarily* dehumanises the slave, is indeed quite lazy (though one might certainly argue that it still *could* illustrate a degree of condescension). More importantly, ancient slavery survived for over a millennium. We shall see that even Marxist historians believed that this implied the co-option of at least some of the slaves, and therefore a softening of the potential logic of the slave's status as property. Kudlien was therefore surely correct when he suggested that (in effect) fear and loathing are not entirely predominant in these texts. But, again, showing that does not in any way prove its opposite. It does not 'prove' a 'positive' view of slave life. Nastiness may be only 'part' of the picture, but how big a part?

It would, nonetheless, be criminal if Anglophone scholarship (with notable exceptions such as the late Thomas Wiedemann) continued to downplay the work of the Mainz *Forschungen*. That would be to disregard the variety of approaches actually adopted by its authors. Secondly, it would waste an astonishing collection of often little-known evidence. Thirdly, it would deprive us of perspectives that can often serve as challenges to our own sometimes lazy orthodoxies. Lastly, we shall see throughout the book that whatever the faults of individual authors within the *Forschungen*, they are equally mirrored in the faults of those who have criticised it (including myself). Let us turn now, however, to an utterly different reading of ancient slavery, one which will also introduce us to some of the themes that will dominate the remainder of this book.

Garrido-Hory and the 'Besançon' school

Germany was not the only country with a major research project into ancient slavery. French scholars began to develop their own approach with a series of publications associated with Besançon. Their work is today most obviously represented by the conferences of GIREA, the Groupe Internationale de Recherche sur l'Esclavage dans l'Antiquité (International Group for Research on Ancient Slavery). GIREA XXIX is currently being published. Their work can also be seen in the *Dialogues d'Histoire Ancienne* and a number of monographs. As with the Mainz project it would be easy to exaggerate the cohesiveness or uniformity of the approach. There is, however, a general emphasis upon

41

investigating the way ancient authors thought about slavery and the ideas that they associated with it. 'Besançon' scholars did not share the functionalist approach of some of the Mainz work, often leaning instead towards theories stressing the more negative side of slave life and the conflicts within societies based on slavery. No one piece of work will give a full flavour of their work, but Marguerite Garrido-Hory's monographs on slaves and ex-slaves in the poems of Juvenal and Martial help illustrate perhaps the most distinctive (but not necessarily *typical*) element of the 'Besançon' work, the development of the 'Index Thématique'. This was a sophisticated indexing system designed to assist the cataloguing of concepts used in association with slavery in ancient texts. It helped ensure that different scholars contributing to the project provided comparable results and it also allowed statistical analyses. Discussions of ancient authors requiring pie-charts and columns of terms can, however, appear a little daunting to the uninitiated and may help explain why this group, like the Mainz scholars, has never quite had the impact on Anglophone scholarship it deserves.

Garrido-Hory chose to examine the writings of Martial and Juvenal who lived in Rome around AD 50-130 (Garrido-Hory 1981, 1998). The concentration on individual authors is vitally important. Roman writers wrote philosophy, history, comedy, satire and other types of texts, and the image of the slave one finds in their work can differ dramatically according to genre. Research such as Garrido-Hory's provides the best opportunity of spotting the differences. The concentration by Garrido-Hory and others on individual authors also offers us our best hope of discovering how the Romans *thought* about slavery, something affecting virtually every piece of evidence surviving from Antiquity. Her work is an astonishing resource. One can track down (for example) every reference to the clothes of a slave in Juvenal (1998: 567), or every reference to the geographical origin of a slave in Martial (1981: 75-6). One can even discover what 'Danubian' might have meant to a Roman author whenever a slave from the Danube region was mentioned (1998: 201). The discussions of slavery terminology are of fundamental importance (1981: ch. 3, 1998: 59-75). The indices stand as a major achievement on their own regardless of any conclusions drawn from them. The 'Index Thématique' approach is, however, a method, not a theory. Interpretation must follow data-gathering, and interpretation, as we have already seen, is a messy business.

Garrido-Hory noted that the slaves we meet in the *Satires* of Juvenal and the poems of Martial are a very skewed sample. They appeared mostly in a domestic, urban, luxury context, reflecting the poets' interest in the homes of the super-wealthy. Young male slaves predominate, often mentioned in a sexual context. Agricultural slaves appeared only in passing (see e.g. 1981: ch. 5, 1998: 99-105, 112-28). There was no disquiet about the institution of slavery (1981: 225, 1998: 217). Slaves were seen as objects. References to slaves who carried their masters on litters distinguished them little from the litter itself (1981: 38, 1998: 174). The possibility of social mobility was mentioned, but successful ex-slaves were generally pilloried. They were competitors for the support of rich patrons upon whom many poor freeborn Romans were dependent (1981: 176-9, 1998: 152-8, 194-5).

I want to focus, however, on two areas where Garrido-Hory's interpretation of slavery differs dramatically from Kudlien's, notably her assessment of the level of oppression suffered by slaves and the accompanying level of resistance.

Garrido-Hory made much of a series of passages in Martial where slaves are subject to vicious physical abuse (1981: 92-3, and esp. 173-4). The use of the whip was 'courante' (1981: 173). Similar passages could be found in Juvenal's poems, but Garrido-Hory noted more of a discussion there of the acceptable limits of mistreatment. With reference to texts such as *Satires* 6.474-85, she argued (1998: 138):

> The whip and the rod are the most current instruments of punishment but if one strikes or beats slaves in the *Satires* it is always injudiciously, to punish minor faults – a slave who is late, a curl of hair misplaced, the theft of a cake – which allows Juvenal to denounce cruelty, even the irrationality of owners, particularly women, without calling the use of corporal punishment into question, but showing the dangers, in the first place the risk of rousing the hatred of the oppressed who could presently avenge themselves on their master by spreading scandal.

We shall see, however, that criticism of bad masters is common to both Martial and Juvenal. In addition, the motivation for such criticism may not be as cynical as Garrido-Hory claims. The references to punishment in Martial come in one of two types. Many are critical of owners who punish for insufficient or unfair reasons. A cook is beaten

for undercooking the meat (*Epigrams* 3.13 and 3.94). A slave
is flogged for allegedly failing to pass on an invitation to
dinner that the embarrassed master had never actually sent
(*Epigrams* 7.86). Other references to punishment may be
more neutral (*Epigrams* 3.21 and 10.56 on branding,
Epigrams 9.22 and 10.56 on fettering, 14.79 on whipping).
So, while Garrido-Hory is quite right to argue that Martial
never calls into question the validity of corporal punishment,
it could be argued nonetheless that he highlighted a series of
situations where masters (and mistresses) had gone *too far*. If
Epigrams 2.66 can be used as an example of the prevalence of
punishment for minor errors (1981: 174n46), is it not also
significant that Lalage, the owner, is *condemned* for acting in
this way? True, 'Martial' himself cheerfully tells us that he
whipped his cook for preparing a bad meal (*Epigrams* 8.23),
but how might the poet have expected his audience to have
reacted to this? With approval? Surprise? Distaste? Martial is
explicit elsewhere that one should not simply presume the
morals of the poems are his own (*Epigrams* 11.15). He can
operate 'in character', and that character might have been
seen as shocking. *Both* Martial and Juvenal, therefore, were
involved in negotiating the limits of abuse.

Garrido-Hory stressed the general passivity of slaves (see
e.g. 1981: 178), but we have just seen that she, at the same
time, argued that fear of slave retaliation was a major spur to
slaveowners to prevent abuse. The master 'lived in fear of
treachery, the harshness of repression carrying within it the
seeds of rebellion' (1998: 62). How great was this fear, in
either Juvenal's or Martial's work?

In one poem Martial tells the story of the crucifixion of the highwayman Laureolus (*Spectacles* 7). This punishment was sometimes re-enacted in the arena. Garrido-Hory saw the need for such horror as indicative of the fear of slave rebellion (1981: 174). She has a point: Martial indeed stated that it was the proper fate for a slave who had stabbed his master. Martial then, however, explains that it was appropriate also for anyone who had stabbed a parent, robbed a temple, or tried to burn down Rome. It therefore indicates that killing one's master was regarded as among the foulest of crimes, but it gives no indication how common this was or how great the attendant fear. Therefore Garrido-Hory's suggestion that the whole gory scenario was a response to threats to the 'ordre sociale esclavagiste' potentially exaggerates how seriously the threat was perceived. This is also true of her insistence on the alleged fear of the (slave) barber's knife (1981: 142-3). Of Martial's references to the 'danger' of slave barbers one is simply an attack on an *unskilled* barber who cuts his customers to pieces (*Epigrams* 11.84). Another features someone who uses (unmanly) depilatories (*Epigrams* 7.83). Is he, asks Martial sarcastically, afraid of the barber? Roman slaveowners' apparent continued willingness to use slave barbers suggests the man was hardly representative. Only once is there a suggestion that a slave barber would consciously abuse his position (*Epigrams* 11.58). The poem complains that the slave-boy favourite Telesphorus is demanding too much and denying his master his sexual pleasures. He may think he is getting away with it, but what, Martial speculates, if his slave-barber were to use his razor to demand his freedom? He would make the promise and then, once safe, have the barber's legs and hands broken.

Telesphorus had better get the point. Is Martial's 'fear' of his barber here meant to sound reasonable or absurd? For a final example of a physical fear of slaves, there is a reference to a possible poisoning (*Epigrams* 12.91). Does this one poem mean that the Romans lived in dread of poison (Garrido-Hory 1981: 173)?

There were, of course, other sources of fear. Slaves might use their knowledge of their master to spread malicious gossip about him. In Martial we hear that deaf slaves are sometimes preferred to the hearing and one slave has his cut tongue out before crucifixion to stop him talking (1981: 92 and esp. 174 with reference to *Epigrams* 2.82, cf. 11.38 and 12.24). Garrido-Hory also saw evidence for this in Juvenal (1998: 62, 116, 138). Here, for example, is *Satires* 9:102ff.:

O Corydon, Corydon, do you think that there can be any secret for a rich man? Even though the slaves are silent the carriage horses will talk, and the dog, and the door and the marble floor. ... For what accusation do slaves not hesitate to bring against their masters, how often do they avenge the strap with gossip? ... Life should be lived properly for many reasons, but chiefly and especially for this: so as not to be concerned for the tongues of one's servants.

The suggestion, however, is that only the *guilty* live in fear. There is no suggestion here that brutal (but socially respectable) masters should worry. The cutting out of a slave's tongue in Martial is also seen as admission of shameful guilt (*Epigrams* 2.82). There is no necessary proof of a general 'fear' here.

Romans may have recognised the need to control the mistreatment of slaves in order to ensure the safety of owners, but Juvenal generally seems little concerned with this connection. *Satires* 6.475-95, where a woman is criticised for the vicious and unwarranted treatment of her household, gives no hint of it. Garrido-Hory only mentioned this passage in a footnote (1998: 138n209). She quoted the following passage from the same poem, but without teasing out the potential implications (1998: 138). Juvenal complains of the evils of women. He imagines a wife demanding the following from her husband (6.219-24):

'Put the slave on the cross.' 'But by what crime has the slave earned execution? What witness comes forward? Who accused him? Give him a hearing: no delay is ever [too] long when it concerns the execution of a man.' 'Madman, so a slave is a man? He has done nothing, so be it: I want this, I order it, let my will serve as reason.' And so she gives orders to her husband.

The wife's attitude to the slave is portrayed as unreasonable in itself, not because of its consequences. One might compare *Satires* 14.15-26 which discusses the impact of the character of Rutilius upon his son. Rutilius is a little too happy with shackles and brandings, whipping and torture. He is, we are told, hardly teaching his son patience, nor that the bodies of slave and free are 'composed of the same elements'. He is, instead, teaching his son 'to give vent to his rage', just as Larga is teaching her daughter to be an adultress. The moral of the story is that children will follow us in our 'crimina' if we teach them to (14.38-40). Cruelty to the slaves and adultery are here then bracketed as similar 'faults'. In other passages, skinflints and wastrels are criticised for not seeing to the material needs of their slaves (*Satires* 1.93 and 14.126-7). The criticisms are not directed primarily towards wastefulness or the reaction that this type of imagined behaviour might incite in slaves: it seems something wrong in and of itself. Garrido-Hory may be correct that a fear of potential retribution lay behind Roman calls for the better treatment of slaves, but these texts hardly make her case. Indeed, Juvenal (and Martial) could instead be read as implying a Roman debate about the limits of the mistreatment of slaves, even as their writings also illustrate the extent of possible abuses. This, however, is not the kind of story that Garrido-Hory sought from her evidence, any more than Kudlien had wished to emphasise the inhumanity of master towards slave from his.

The differences in tone (but similarities in method) between Kudlien and Garrido-Hory can also be seen in the latter's treatment of emotional ties between masters and slaves. We find a series of epitaphs in Martial for favourite slaves, e.g. the young girl Erotion (*Epigrams* 5.37). Garrido-Hory argued that these favourites were valued largely as luxury objects (though one might counter that 'epitaphs' for favourite animals appear rarely, e.g. *Epigrams* 1.109 and 11.69). Garrido-Hory also suggested that the sentiments towards Erotion represented a exceptional case (1981: 119), though that had not prevented her from using evidence from a single poem to argue a fear of slave barbers (see above). If it is true, as Garrido-Hory stressed, that the position of slave 'favourite' lasted only while the slave was sexually attractive (in effect still a child), Martial nonetheless sometimes expressed something of a bad conscience about their later fate: sending one to work in the kitchen was obviously not the 'done thing' (*Epigrams* 10.66). We need to be careful, however: I am not claiming on the basis of such cases that Garrido-Hory is wrong to stress the utter inhumanity of slavery. These slaves were sexually abused. They were seen as objects. I wish, however, to illustrate some of the problems and assumptions behind her interpretations. She wrote (1981: 171, cf. 1981: 224):

> Behind the incontestable sincerity of the sentiments which show that these desired slaves were able to awaken in their masters lies, however, the image of the slave-as-object of luxury and pleasure which by its presence bore witness of the wealth of the master and his elevated position in the dominant class.

One could, just as easily, have reversed the sentence (in the style of some of the Mainz *Forschungen*) and suggested that whereas slaves were indeed seen as luxury possessions, behind *that* lay a reality of affective, human relations. Both positions can be argued on the basis of the available evidence.

Overall, Garrido-Hory's evidence of tension and fear can be made to look less impressive than it appeared at first sight. This is not, of course, to deny that there was such tension and fear in reality, but just to point out that Martial and Juvenal are not necessarily good evidence for it. One might argue that since satire was an essentially comic genre, slave resistance might have been deliberately edited out of the poems. As with

2. Ancient Slavery and Modern Geography

Kudlien's interpretation of oracles, the nature of the evidence therefore allows the historian to produce a range of very different interpretations. We have horror stories from Martial and Juvenal, but it is difficult to know exactly how we should read them. Does one regard the stories about slaves in the *Epigrams* and *Satires* as representative of typical abuses which moral objections did nothing to stop? Or as examples of stories horrific to Romans, not just to us? Were they the product of a society attempting to police itself through non-legal social expectations, setting limits to the acceptable mistreatment of slaves? No index in the world, no matter how sophisticated, will give us the answer.

Thus far we have examined a generally positive image of the lives of slaves (Kudlien) and a more negative one (Garrido-Hory), and showed some of the problems with both. The difficulty, however, is that we can't just halve the difference or come up with some 'middle ground'. As we will see when we turn to look at some of the most sophisticated global readings of slavery ever produced, this problem is not connected with *individual* historians of ancient slavery, but with the very idea of producing a narrative of Roman slave life.

3

Struggling with Class: Shtaerman, Trofimova and a Marxist View of Roman Slavery and Agriculture

Marxism has proven a major impetus to the study of ancient slavery, but is quite difficult to define (see McKeown 1999). There is a fairly predictable body of Marxist language, notably 'mode of production', 'forces of production', 'relations of production' and especially 'class' and 'class conflict'. The emphasis given to various elements, however, and their precise meanings (both individually and in combination), are often effectively decided by individual historians. Marx himself, for example, may have stressed the importance of class conflict, but famously nowhere precisely defined class. This is not to say that it cannot be defined (or even that one cannot suggest a definition that Marx himself might have accepted), but one should not expect any kind of orthodoxy by which 'Marxist' authors can be compared to one another, or even clearly differentiated from non-Marxists. If Marxist historiography is, as some have suggested, best understood as a language common to a number of historians, it is a language without any agreed dictionary.

3. Struggling with Class

Some examples can help illustrate this. Geoffrey de Ste. Croix's monumental and passionate *The Class Struggle in the Ancient Greek World* defined class struggle as economic exploitation and resistance to it (1983: 42-69). He surveyed what he saw as a largely one-sided class struggle between the unfree (not just chattel slaves) and the propertied elite in the Classical world and sought to show its long-term impact on the decline of Greek democracy and on the fall of the Roman empire (1983: 300ff., 453ff.). The work is an astonishing collection of ancient examples of the exploitation of individuals and of groups. Italian Marxists writing about the slave mode of production viewed the phenomenon in a very different manner, however (Giardina and Schiavone 1981a-c). They examined how slavery impacted on the rest of society, and the bulk of their work sought to trace the archaeological footprint of slavery on the economy of Rome in the late republic and the early empire. The slaves themselves appear almost as abstractions. In France, Jean-Pierre Vernant argued that in classical Greece slaves never achieved the group-consciousness that would have allowed them to be part of the class struggle (Vernant 1980). Vernant was then free largely to ignore them in the rest of his work (though this has not been true of the work of French authors working under the GIREA umbrella, who were certainly influenced by Marxist thinking). These are all massively different (but equally fascinating) 'Marxist' approaches to the same problem. Even Soviet Marxist historiography, where one might expect to see more conformity, witnessed serious disagreements and changes of interpretation (see e.g. Raskolnikoff 1975 and Mazza 1975).

If one were to attempt an intentionally vague definition that might cover *most* Marxist historians it would probably include (a) explicit appeal to Marx's ideas, (b) the use of some of the Marxist 'language' mentioned above, (c) an interest in exploited groups (in antiquity largely, but not exclusively, slaves) and how they are controlled, and (d) a particular emphasis on tensions within society, how they are manifested ideologically and the way in which those tensions created change.

Shtaerman and Trofimova's argument

Shtaerman (or Staerman) and Trofimova's work on slavery in the early Roman empire provides an excellent study of a 'Marxist' approach. It satisfies all four of my conditions. It also remains one of the very finest books written on ancient slavery (though the Italian translation of 1975 is the only non-Russian edition). It combined a clear theoretical commitment with an encyclopaedic knowledge of the sources. Shtaerman and Trofimova set out to explain a particularly important change in Roman society. In the early Roman empire rich farmers directly exploited slave gangs. By the end of the empire they appear to have switched largely to using sharecropping tenants (*coloni*). These were tied to the land but their precise legal status, whether free or slave, was of secondary importance. Formerly free cultivators might have suffered with the change, but slaves may have found more independence and greater chances of creating a family. Shtaerman and Trofimova's explanation of these events forms perhaps the most sophisticated and wide-ranging argument ever produced on ancient slavery which continues to have an impact (particularly in Italy and France) long after its publication.

I want to summarise a sample of their evidence. Then I want to turn that evidence on its head, showing how it could be used to argue a very different case. Why would I wish to do that? Because I can – and the fact that I can may have important implications for how we understand ancient slavery and, more generally, the past.

'Class struggle' was at the forefront of Shtaerman and Trofimova's explanation of social change in the Roman empire (1975: 183):

The abyss dividing masters from slaves and poor working classes from upper classes became noticeably deeper from that existing in previous centuries. The contemptuous disdain on the one side, and the repressed hatred on the other, which exploded every now and again, characterised the relationship between rulers and ruled.

A superficial observer receives the impression that the position of the main exploited classes is improving, that the contradictions are softened, but in reality, beneath the apparent reconciliation is ripening the explosion called forth to put an end to that mode of production (249).

Let us look at their explanation of that 'explosion'. They cited a vast and persuasive array of evidence, but, having summarised it, we will ask, once more, what may happen if we do not share their starting assumptions.

They argued (1975: ch. 2) that Roman sources perceived a growing difficulty in the control of agricultural slaves as early as the first century AD. They noted that Columella, writing at the time, warned that poorly supervised slaves could ruin a farm (*On Agriculture* esp. 1.7.3 and 1.7.6). Ideally, slaves should be watched by their master (1.1.18), but Columella recognised that this might be impractical. A slave manager, or *vilicus*, should be trained, preferably from an early age (1.8 and 11.1.2-29). He must be a leader without being cruel, and mild without being manipulated by his workforce. He must learn all the skills of the farm, rise before the other workers, be free from vice, etc. Most importantly he must be utterly loyal to his master (11.1.7). Without that, all other virtues were worthless. Shtaerman and Trofimova argued that Columella's loyal *vilicus* is a fantasy figure: Columella himself noted that an illiterate slave-manager might be no bad thing because he was less likely to defraud the farm owner (1.8.4). So much for total loyalty! Romans were, Shtaerman and Trofimova believed, generally increasingly distrustful of educated slaves (1975: 5, 38-40, 227-8). The amount of supervision on farms grew without a corresponding increase in productivity (if anything, Shtaerman and Trofimova suggest a decrease: 36-7). Legal texts mentioning debts incurred by managers and sub-letters showed that the option of indirect control also failed to address the basic problem (68). Extra layers of unproductive management only made things worse. Columella's solutions to the problems of slave agriculture were therefore 'utopian' (9, 37). They were unlikely to help even with estates with a few dozen slaves and were utterly impractical on even larger farms (9). This would soon become crucial.

The problems with agricultural slaves were allegedly part of a much bigger picture. Divisions between master and slave were widening (Shtaerman and Trofimova 1975: ch. 6). Cato the Elder had been willing to dine with his slaves around 200 BC (Plutarch, *Cato the Elder* 3). Two hundred and fifty years later the supposedly humanitarian philosopher Seneca the Younger felt it an insult even to be asked to do so (*On the Firmness of the Wise Man* 15). Writers such as Pliny the Younger (*c.* AD 100) expressed a fear of slaves (Pliny *Letters* 3.14.5). Seneca complained that owners made slaves into enemies (Seneca *Letters* 47.5). A law known as the *senatus consultum Silanianum* demanded the death of the whole slave household of a master who had died in mysterious circumstances (e.g. *Digest* 29.5). The terroristic intent and repeated widening of the scope of this law, Shtaerman and Trofimova suggested, indicated the commonness of the murder of slaveowners (1975: 255). They collected a whole series of literary references to more general forms of resistance including flight, suicide and self-harm (256-8, 269-70). A whole series of new laws were introduced to deal with runaway slaves (230-1, citing *Digest* 11.3-4). There were also indirect indicators of the severity of the class struggle. Slaves were gradually offered some protection under Roman law (196ff., 214ff., 242ff.). For example, sick slaves abandoned to die could not be re-enslaved if they survived (Suetonius, *Claudius* 25, cf. *Digest* 40.8.2). The state recognised a need to restrain cruelty in order to prevent disorder (*Mosaicorum et Romanarum legum* coll 3.3, Gaius, *Institutes* 1.58-9). While the definition of 'unjustifiable' cruelty remained vague, and while slaveowners would have been judged by other slaveowners, these rights for slaves were not just hypothetical. Shtaerman and Trofimova argued that elites give concessions only when forced to do so (1975: 252). They also suggested that such laws reduced the profitability of slave exploitation just a little, further helping to undermine it (251). As a second indirect indicator of conflict Shtaerman and Trofimova noted an increasing attempt to portray the relationship between master and slave as paternalistic, e.g. with the spread of stories of loyalty from slaves in times of crisis (200-3: e.g. Appian *Civil Wars* 4.6.43-8). This was part of a desperate attempt to maintain the control of slaves by making them 'internalise' the values of their masters. It failed. Many slaves turned instead to movements such as Christianity which rejected the world and values of their oppressors (Shtaerman and Trofimova 1975: ch. 9, e.g. 280). Many slaves looked now to the world of Christ, not the world of Caesar.

This alleged growing gap between master and slave became vital because of other changes Shtaerman and Trofimova believed were happening. The peace which followed the end of the civil wars in Rome in the first century BC saw a growth both in cities and in the imperial bureaucracy (notably the creation of a standing army). Landowners were expected to finance the bureaucracy and supply cities with amenities and (sometimes) cheap food (Shtaerman and Trofimova 1975: 8, 251, 327-8). Even without traditional land taxes, burdens therefore grew, particularly on small and medium landowners in Italy. The new legal rights for slaves cut the profits of these landowners. At the same time, the growth of taxation in kind began to restrict market production. Market production (e.g. of wine and olive oil) had previously provided the best opportunity for estate owners to make the profits required to balance the costs of acquiring their slaves and maintaining them all year round. These markets had previously also allowed them to procure easily both slaves and many of the items (e.g. clothes) required to support their workforce. The growing restriction in market production therefore hit them hard. Larger estates had fewer difficulties with the changes. They were more able to produce what they needed for themselves (334) and were also more able to protect themselves from encroachment by the state and its tax raising officials. The less economic small to medium farms therefore started to give way to bigger farms. The new, bigger, estates gradually moved away from the exploitation of slave labour. The Romans, as we have seen Shtaerman and Trofimova argue, were supposedly already having serious difficulties controlling their slaves. Concentrating even greater numbers on large estates would only have made them more dangerous. Large landowners turned instead to a different labour system. Tenants, free or slave, would be allowed to keep part of their crop as an incentive and were to be left to maintain themselves, thus removing much of the need for expensive supervision. The 'colonate' was born. Shtaerman and Trofimova believed their explanation of its birth was better than the alternatives. There was no evidence farmers moved away from slave labour because slave supplies were dwindling (ch. 1). There is also no evidence that technological advances had driven the change, requiring a more motivated or better trained workforce than slaves could offer. The colonate was, if anything, technologically more primitive than the slave system it replaced (4).

Another way of reading the same evidence

Let us examine what happens when we re-read a small sample of Shtaerman and Trofimova's evidence, but with a different starting assumption. Let us imagine that there was no 'crisis' and that slave/ master relations were actually no worse in the imperial period than before.

Were rural slaves becoming more difficult to exploit? Not necessarily. Firstly, slaveowners of all periods seem to have had a tendency to complain about the laziness of their slaves. Cato the Elder, writing two hundred years *before* Columella, warned his readers of the kind of excuses managers might use for poor work on the farm (*On Agriculture* 2). Secondly, if Romans complained about slaves, they also complained about free labourers and tenants (e.g. Pliny the Younger, *Letters* 9.37, cf. Columella himself, *On Agriculture* 1.7). Lastly, while Pliny the Elder famously suggested that the largest slave-run farms, the *latifundia*, were 'the ruin of Italy' (*Natural Histories* 18.7.35), few wealthy Romans seem to have retired to work a tiny two-*iugera* farm by the sweat of their own brow like the men of yore (Juvenal, *Satires* 14.156ff.). We might note that Pliny also claimed that doctors, mainly conquered Greeks, were trying to murder Romans one by one and get paid for it (*Natural Histories* 29.7). The continuing popularity of Greek medicine suggests that Pliny is not necessarily the best representative of upper-class Roman thought.

Shtaerman and Trofimova admitted that our statistical evidence is so poor we cannot be sure whether productivity was falling, stable, or rising in relative or absolute terms (1975: 333-4). None of our major sources Cato (*c.* 200-150 BC), Varro (*c.* 50 BC) and Columella (*c.* 50 AD) was trying to write an economic treatise in a modern sense. One could argue that there is a trend from Cato to Columella towards increasing levels of supervision of slave labour, but judging a trend from just three surviving authors is dangerous. The differences in the level of supervision suggested may represent their individual preferences rather than changes over time. Columella, for instance, praised Xenophon's *Oeconomicus*, a Greek philosophical text that saw activity and supervision as good things *in themselves* (*On Agriculture* 11.1.5). It is clear from Varro that Roman authors whose works have *not* survived may have had very different views on the level of slave productivity and supervision: *On Agriculture* 1.18. Shtaerman and Trofimova admit themselves that Columella's statistics were in contradiction to a handful surviving from his contemporary Pliny the Elder (1975: 37).

Even if management input did increase over time, need this imply a crisis? The change away from slavery need not indicate that there was one. There were, as we shall see, other possible reasons for the change. Might not extra management have paid for itself by increasing production? Shtaerman and Trofimova argued that there is no evidence that it did, but this is not the same as proving that it did not, especially given the weaknesses of our evidence. Legal sources discussing the indebtedness of managers and sub-letters (for example) need not imply that these forms of middle management *generally* failed (Shtaerman and Trofimova 1975: 67-8). It only shows that they *sometimes* failed or *could* fail and that this was of interest to lawyers. One *could* take the view that middle management became such an important legal subject because it was popular and, implicitly, a success!

There is, in fact, a crucial problem with Shtaerman and Trofimova's argument that rural slavery was in crisis. They used Columella to illustrate the problems facing Roman slaveowners but ignored the fact that Columella clearly felt that he was offering entirely sensible solutions to those problems. Much of his advice regarding slave farm managers (for example, that they avoid the company of strangers or getting involved in religious cults) seems more like pragmatism than 'utopianism' (cf. *On Agriculture* 1.8.10 on the need to develop virtues 'as much as his slavish nature allows'). Yes, Columella wanted his manager to be as wise and well-trained as possible, but surely perfection is an acceptable aim. Arguing that loyalty was a key virtue hardly means that it is unrealisable. The comment that a farm manager *might* be illiterate does not mean that Columella was suggesting that they *should* be. He was suggesting that *even* an illiterate slave could do the job, and quoted Celsus, who noted (possibly entirely rhetorically) that it might be an advantage in preventing fraud. Columella believed that farming would be profitable and that a watched slave *would* work satisfactorily (e.g. 1.8.11, 1.9.4-8).

The increasing distrust of *any* kind of educated slaves alleged by Shtaerman and Trofimova may also be exaggerated.

3. Struggling with Class

One could argue that such distrust was a permanent element in Roman society, not a new phenomenon (witness the figure of the 'cunning slave' in the comedies of Plautus *c.* 200 BC, discussed in Chapter 5 below). If there were fewer prominent slave intellectuals under the empire, this may have had nothing to do with 'distrust'. The conquest of the eastern Mediterranean in the late republic had (a) closed off a major supply route supply of skilled, intellectual captives and (b) eventually opened up Rome to a pool of skilled *free* intellectuals from the same area during the early empire (Shtaerman and Trofimova 1975: 144). Intellectual slaves were therefore less needed. In any case, given the complaints of some imperial authors about slave doctors and educators, the disappearance of slave intellectuals may be exaggerated (as Shtaerman and Trofimova came close to accepting, 331). Finally, Columella was more than happy to train agricultural slaves *in agriculture*. How far did the lack of slave playwrights (to take just an example) affect the profitability of *farms*? In general Roman slaveowners were much less worried about their slaves gaining an education than, for example, American slaveowners were to be.

Finally, *even if* controlling large groups of slaves had become problematic (for which we have seen little proof), Shtaerman and Trofimova fail to explain why large owners could not have continued to manage their properties as a collection of smaller units (which they mentioned as a pattern of land use occurring earlier in Roman history: 10). The unit of management need not equate with the unit of ownership: they could be subdivided.

Let us move now from agriculture to the overall relations

between slave and free. Shtaerman and Trofimova suggested an acute and growing crisis there too. Let us re-examine some of the key evidence there.

Cato the Elder (*floruit c.* 200-150 BC) had indeed dined with his slaves, and Seneca the Younger, *c.* 50 AD, could indeed find the idea insulting. Do we therefore have proof of a growing divide between slave and free? Not necessarily. Leaving aside the fact that Seneca actually *recommended* dining with slaves on one occasion (*Letters* 47.2), Cato is an odd choice to illustrate early Roman 'paternalism'. Cato's second-century AD biographer regarded him as a byword for an uncaring master who could drive his slaves to suicide (Plutarch, *Cato the Elder* 10), even if he did raise slaves like his own children. In his *On Agriculture* Cato recommended that rations should be cut for sick slaves and, where possible, the sick and ill should be sold (2). Food and clothing for labourers (56-9) were discussed between sections discussing feed for cattle (54 and 60). If one wanted to, one could use the evidence of Cato to suggest that the divide between slave and free was decreasing, not increasing, over time. We need to be careful with anecdote.

What of the growing *fear* of slaves? Pliny the Younger famously described the murder of a man by his slaves. The man had been cruel, but Pliny seems to suggest that everyone needs to be on their guard (*Letters* 3.14). Mildness, apparently, could not guarantee a master's safety. This, however, did not prevent Pliny from wanting to portray himself elsewhere as a mild master who shows concern for his 'people' (*Letters* 4.10, 5.6, 5.19, 6.3, 8.1, 8.16, 8.19, cf. 9.21 and 9.24). There is little to suggest he feared his own slaves.

Pliny mentioned two episodes where masters died in mysterious circumstances (*Letters* 6.25, 8.14, cf. 7.6). There is no sense of panic, nor even an assumption that the slaves were responsible. He even intervened to ensure that the freedmen of one of the dead men should *not* be executed alongside his slaves, suggesting that the need for 'deterrence' was not always foremost in his thoughts.

If, however, Pliny was relatively unworried, why did he write in *Letter* 3.14 that no master could be safe? We are told that the dead man, Larcius Macedo, was the son of an ex-slave. Pliny felt this perhaps explained his uncouth cruelty towards his slaves. Pliny's willingness to give all the gory details of Macedo's death seems contrary to his protestation that it was not the kind of thing one should put in a letter. The moral drawn, that none of us is safe, is strangely at odds with a narrative clearly implying that Macedo helped bring his fate upon himself. Pliny then explains how Macedo was once humiliated in a public bath-house when a social inferior had (accidentally) struck him like a slave. As I have discussed in detail elsewhere (McKeown: forthcoming (a)), Pliny's 'moral' to the tale starts to look more and more ironic. There may be more snobbery here than fear (cf. Pliny's contempt of the ex-slave Pallas, *Letters* 7.29, 8.6). Such an ironic reading of this material would solve Shtaerman and Trofimova's 'difficulty' with Pliny, that he mixed (in their opinion) a generally genial attitude towards slaves with a paranoid fear of them here (1975: 203). Perhaps his fear need not be taken too seriously.

What, however, of the famous adage quoted by Seneca that we have 'as many enemies as we have slaves'? Here is

Shtaerman and Trofimova's summary of Seneca's *Letter* 47 where that remark is found (1975: 196):

> The base idea, ... is that, when a master ran the risk of being killed or denounced by his slaves and when reversals of fortune and the will of the emperor made possible the elevation on high of a slave and the humiliation of a master, cruelty and intimidation are bad helpers.

There is no denying that the picture given of slave/ master relations in *Letter* 47 is bleak, but we should bear in mind that Seneca obviously hoped his audience would find it *unacceptably* so: he wanted to shock. Seneca criticises slaveowners who will not eat with their servants but demand that they stand silent (and hungry), ready to clean up their master's vomit. This attitude, Seneca suggests, is both ludicrous and dangerous. Slaves allowed to talk at dinner do not gossip about their master behind his back: they even keep silent under torture. He notes (47.5):

> Then there is that proverb which originates from the same arrogant attitude, that we have as many enemies as we have slaves. They aren't our enemies unless we make them so.

When, therefore, Seneca talks about 'as many enemies as slaves' he may not be making a comment on slaves, but on a certain type of master. For Seneca this saying is the motto of the inhumane, those whose attitudes are to avoided and should be revolting to decent Romans. When Seneca thinks about slaves he usually thinks about their *powerlessness*, not their hostility (e.g. *On Anger* 2.21.3-4, 3.4.4, 3.17.1, *On Benefits* 1.2.5, 3.18.1, *On Mercy* 1.18.1). Indeed, in a seldom-quoted section of *Letters* 47 (47.20) slaveowners are warned they should avoid acting like tyrants. Tyrants forget the powerlessness of others and, even though they cannot be harmed invent harms done to them so they can hurt and punish others. The class war is one-sided here: slaves are on the receiving end. Seneca does sometimes suggest that even the most powerful should remember that the powerful can be brought down by the lowly, the master by the slave (*On Anger* 1.2.2, 1.3.2, 2.11.4, *On Mercy* 1.26.1, *Letters* 4.8). Such statements, however, may be coded statements to the emperor about his relationship with aristocrats such as Seneca (e.g. *On Anger* 3.16), and it may be the very surprise the comment produces that he finds attractive as a writer.

Surely, however, the *senatus consultum Silanianum*, ordering the killing of the household of a master who had died mysteriously, implies that only terrorism could keep slaves under control? Why else kill all the domestic slaves unless one wanted give them a strong incentive to expose any plots against their masters for fear of the possible repercussions? Again, not necessarily. The law itself is recorded under Roman inheritance law: the very need to require heirs to kill the slaves implies some were tempted to put profit before vengeance or intimidation. Secondly, the law affected only slaves who had failed to help a master who had been physically attacked. If a master was killed by poison, for example, the poisoner was punished, but not the whole household (*Digest* 29.5.1.18).

This is an odd exception if the aim of the law was to encourage slaves to inform on dangers to their master. It suggests a narrower aim of ensuring that slaves didn't put their own safety before that of their owners. Thirdly, changes in the law were not exclusively – or even mainly – in the direction of increasing harshness (see e.g. *Digest* 29.5.1.5, 29.5.1.30-2 with 29.5.14, 29.5.3.pr., 29.5.3.7, exempting deaf slaves, the dumb, children, etc.). The attention devoted over time to this piece of legislation need not imply that the relationship between master and slave was somehow worsening or that murder of masters by slaves was necessarily more common than, for example, parricide (just as shocking, but raising fewer complicated property issues).

During the reign of Nero in the first century AD, Pedanius Secundus, a high-ranking politician who held the post of City Prefect, was murdered by a slave. Tacitus' report of the 'noteworthy crime' is often cited in support of the 'terroristic' intent of the *SC Silanianum* (*Annals* 14.40-5, esp. 42-5). 'Ancient custom' meant that 400 slaves living in Secundus' urban household should die. Rioting ensued, and the Senate debated the case. Cassius Longinus gave an impassioned and successful speech against leniency, arguing that the only way to control slaves was through intimidation. It should be remembered, however, that Pedanius had been a particularly important man. One of the City Prefect's jobs was, ironically, to keep the slaves (and plebs) under control (see e.g. *Annals* 6.11). In addition, Tacitus, in another context, presented Longinus, the speaker, as a man of (unusual) *severitas* (*Annals* 13.48). So, while the incident *may* illustrate a deep distrust of slaves and a fear of violence at their hands, it *could* also represent an exaggerated response to a particularly shocking crime.

We do, as Shtaerman and Trofimova noted, find reference to other types of serious slave resistance (including flight and suicide) in the works of Seneca and other writers. None of those references can tell us how frequent such behaviour was, however, or whether it was more common than earlier in Roman history (for which we usually lack equivalent evidence). Shtaerman and Trofimova argued, however, that new laws made concerning runaways in the early and middle empire do indicate that increasing slave flight was a symptom of the growing class conflict. Does more legislation imply more runaways? Again, not necessarily. Firstly, as Shtaerman and Trofimova recognised, running away was a staple form of resistance in all slave societies and at all times of Roman history. Secondly, the bulk of surviving Roman legislation and legal opinion *in all fields* was produced in the first three centuries AD. It may therefore represent an increasing interest in the act of legislating rather than reflect a new or growing social problem. Thirdly, the legislation on runaways mostly dealt with free people who helped runaways, not the runaways themselves, who were left to the tender mercies of their masters. The legislation may, therefore, be a response to higher numbers of runaways, but, again, it *need* not be. All that is certain is that the state increasingly wished to legislate to prevent the free from aiding flight. And *that* could explained by growing competition for labour rather than by growing slave resistance.

Shtaerman and Trofimova, of course, argued that legislation protecting slaves might also be a sign of acute class struggle. Do elites ever give away any of their powers and privileges without, on some level, being *forced* to do so? This may seem a powerful argument, particularly to those of us cynical about the political process, but there are several questions that need to be asked. Firstly, how important *was* legislation? Did legislation create and fashion public opinion, or simply reflect it in a new way? When Vedius Pollio tried, at the very beginning of the empire, to feed one of his slaves to his lampreys for breaking a goblet, there was no law to prevent him doing so (see Seneca, *On Anger* 3.40.2-5, *On Mercy* 1.18.2; Pliny, *Natural Histories* 9.39 (77); Dio Cassius 54.23.1-2). Only the anger of the emperor Augustus, present at the scene, saved the servant. The very survival of the story is, however, significant. Anyone who behaved like Vedius could expect considerable odium. This might appear an ineffective control, but one might ask whether imperial legislation had much greater force (someone had to bring cases for the slaves and a magistrate had to find in their favour). As we noted above, the bulk of imperial legislation (just as, oddly, the majority of inscriptions, as we saw in Chapter 1) date from the first to the third centuries AD. The state also started to legislate on other issues including adultery (see e.g. Raditsa 1980). Some emperors may have been taking their honorific title 'father of the fatherland' seriously. The new laws could, therefore, represent a new tendency to legislate, a change in the discourse between state and individual, rather than a change in attitudes towards slaves.

Even if this legislation represented a new trend, there remains the question of how far it necessarily represents the outcome of a 'class struggle'. One or two laws expressly stated that self-protection lay behind some limitations on cruelty, but this need not have been the primary incentive. Putting a cynical gloss on a law may say as much about the rhetoric of convincing the public to obey it as it does about the original motives of the law-makers. It may be unfashionable to argue that philosophical groups such as the Stoics may have influenced legislation, but it may indeed have been the case. Stoics argued that slaves shared a common humanity with their masters and should be treated fairly. Modern scholars have argued that Stoics such as Seneca could be callous towards their own slaves and that there is little evidence to connect his views with any liberal slave laws of his time (see e.g. Bradley 1994: ch. 7; Garnsey 1996: esp. ch. 9; Griffin 1976: ch. 8; Manning 1989). They have further suggested that Stoic beliefs, centred on the internal moral world of the individual, also had the convenient effect of leaving the *institution* of slavery unchallenged. Both charges may be true, but the hypocrisy of individual thinkers need not undermine the impact of their ideas. And even if Stoics concentrated mainly on the world of ideas, this need not mean that those ideas could not, *over time*, affect attitudes and attitudes affect the law (even if they never led to the abolition of slavery, and even if Stoics were more concerned about their own souls than about the lives of their servants).

We saw that Shtaerman and Trofimova argued that new rights for slaves, *whatever* their origins, helped undermine the profitability of slavery by limiting the exploitation of rural workers (and increasing the need to offer slaves material incentives). But how far would slaves living comparatively isolated lives on farms have been affected by the legislation discussed? Secondly, *all* slave systems have witnessed a balancing between terror and concession. What is particularly new or significant about the changes of the early empire? At what point do they constitute a 'crisis'? The shift towards other forms of labour does not prove such a 'crisis'. We shall see that there are ways of explaining it that have little to do with changes in the relationship between masters and slaves. Indeed, what is to stop us from arguing that these 'concessions' actually helped *increase* the level of exploitation? Might they be seen as *successful* interventions in the class struggle helping defuse the kind of overt rebellion that had been so prominent and so costly in the late republic?

Similar difficulties affect Shtaerman and Trofimova's argument that a new stress on the loyalty of slaves indicated the increasing acuteness of the class conflict. This, of course, relies on using apparent evidence of slave loyalty as an indication of massive *dis*loyalty. Even if we accept this (and Seneca, Valerius Maximus and others do seem to believe that the loyal behaviour they praised was unusual), it is questionable, again, quite how new this phenomenon was. All slave systems wrestle with the distinction between the slave as a thing and the slave as a person, and between using coercion and attempting persuasion. Cato the Elder may, as we saw earlier, have been inhumane in his attitude towards sick slaves, but we are told he also brought up slave children with his own to increase their loyalty (Plutarch, *Cato the Elder* 4-5, 20). Plautus wrote the play *The Captives* in the first half of the second century BC. The character of the slave Tyndarus, who swaps places with his master to save him from slavery (discussed in more detail in Chapter 5), is as optimistic a picture of slave loyalty as anything in the 'loyal slave' stories of Seneca two centuries later. In the first century BC Cicero regarded the disloyalty of some of his slaves as a very personal affront (*Letters to Atticus* 7.2.8; see Chapter 4 below). The hope that slaves might internalise their loyalty was not necessarily anything new in the early empire, even if it may have manifested itself in different ways. And, even if we *could* prove that the 'loyal slave stories' etc. do represent a *new* development, we need not share Shtaerman and Trofimova's interpretation of it. 'Internalisation' might, again, represent a *deepening* of the control over the slave, now that overt slave opposition and open rebellion had been crushed. If Shtaerman and Trofimova viewed it as a sign of crisis, might that be at least in part because they wanted to find such signs?

The troubling ease with which some of Shtaerman and Trofimova's arguments can be turned on their head is especially apparent with their discussion of early Christianity. One can recognise the initial attractiveness of their position. Christianity constituted a profound rejection of Roman values. Hence the Roman state first persecuted Christianity, and, eventually, took control of it. The difficulty, as Shtaerman and Trofimova recognised, is that Christianity is a somewhat odd form of social protest. It famously decreed that one should render unto Caesar those things that were Caesar's (Matthew 22.21). This did nothing to lessen the degree to which the elite could exploit the masses. Of course, Shtaerman and Trofimova could (rightly) counter that their point is subtler. The Christian message offered an alternative value system to that which masters wanted slaves to internalise in order to help divert the deepening class conflict.

As they admitted themselves (Shtaerman and Trofimova 1975: 283-4), however, Christianity quickly began to stress the need for slaves to obey their masters (see e.g. Colossians 3.22-4, Ephesians 6.5, Titus 2.9-10, 1 Peter 2:18-23). Slaves might dream of the next world, but were told, firmly, to do their jobs in this. Ste. Croix and others have consequently argued that Christianity was a mechanism of exploitation, not a sign of crisis (Ste. Croix 1975, 1983: 418-41; Kyrtatas 1987, 1995).

If, however, there was no 'crisis' in slave control why did the Romans move eventually from exploiting slaves to exploiting *coloni*? There are, in fact, explanations available which do not depend on assumptions about developments *within* slavery. We have already seen that Shtaerman and Trofimova noted the contraction in the market economy (e.g. 1975: 334). Contraction of these markets might have convinced landowners to move to less intensive forms of agricultural labour, with fewer input costs: tenants who could fend for themselves. This model need not imply that slave resistance was getting more intense, or even that it was at a particularly high level or that masters regarded their slaves as dangerous.

As another possibility one could argue that the key impetus to change was the increased availability of other forms of labour rather than any new difficulties with slaves (Moses Finley 1998: ch. 4, foreshadowed by Shtaerman and Trofimova 1975: 344). The exploitation of indigenous farmers tends to be easier than exploiting slaves (who have to be found, imported, controlled closely and fed). Most societies have used 'serfs' or some other kind of exploited tenants rather than slaves. The development of such exploitative tenancies in Italy may have initially been rendered difficult by the interconnected political and military rights granted to peasants (see Hopkins 1978: chs 1-2). During the Republic they fought Rome's wars and elected her magistrates. Members of the elite who sought to exploit or abuse free farmers could find themselves at the mercy of their votes or, worse, the focus of their anger. From the early empire, however, Rome's legions were increasingly recruited from outside Italy. The political influence of Italian peasants fell accordingly and with it their ability to protect themselves from exploitation. It became easier for landowners to extort surplus from sharecropping tenants than it was from slaves. Roman society returned to the 'default' position of most other societies: a form of tied peasantry.

One could, doubtless, perform the same kind of critical analysis on these alternatives to Shtaerman and Trofimova's model as we have on theirs. It is not, however, my intention here to write a potted history of Roman economic and social history. Rather I want to illustrate that, however authoritative Shtaerman and Trofimova's picture may appear, it owes its authority to a series of assumptions the reader need not share.

The crucial point is this: the alternative models imply that change may have been due less to developments within slavery than to changes in the *context* within which slavery operated. Shtaerman and Trofimova actually implied this in their introduction and conclusion but not in the body of their text. That they apparently recognised other possibilities but still sought to stress the oncoming 'explosion' of the class struggle illustrates how deeply wedded they were to a model which was actually unnecessary to explain the changes they were describing. One could argue that the essentials of the slave system stayed stable (there were always some murders etc., there was always a balance between compromise and terror) but that nothing necessarily proves that the overall control of slaves was becoming more problematical in the early or middle Roman empire. Indeed the Romans may rather have been working out more refined methods of control. The plausibility of much of Shtaerman and Trofimova's position is effectively created by working backwards: the change from slavery *must* indicate a crisis in slavery, therefore authors such as Seneca and Pliny 'prove' the crisis. An author such as Columella, apparently relatively unworried by the allegedly insuperable 'contradictions', is branded as 'utopian'. The general argument gives 'meaning' to isolated pieces of evidence. I have tried to show how that evidence can actually be read in a variety of ways. Shtaerman and Trofimova's book may be the most powerful argument on ancient slavery ever constructed, but that doesn't mean that it gets to where it wants to go. It most certainly shows, however, the ambition and scope of Marxist theory and its ability to generate fascinating hypotheses.

Keith Bradley:
Passionate about Slavery

Keith Bradley's work on Roman slavery forms the foundation of the current Anglophone understanding of the topic. I want to look at some aspects of his 1994 monograph *Slavery and Society at Rome*, with reference also to his 1984 book *Slaves and Masters in the Roman Empire*. He was clear about his aims. Almost all of our evidence about slaves comes from slave owners. Bradley wanted to rescue slaves from the silence imposed by elite writers, to give a voice to the voiceless and dispossessed. He wanted also to help his reader understand what it was like to live as a slave (1994: 180). In doing that, it would be wrong, he argued, to focus on the (minority) of fortunate slaves who gained freedom, wealth, a place in society: the 'visible and vocal' (1994: 180-1). Any attempt to recapture the psychology of the ordinary slave demanded the use of the fullest range of sources, including both comparative sources and one's imagination.

While Bradley recognised the possibility of emotional ties between slave and master and while he accepted that the 'social death' of the slave was sometimes exaggerated in modern historiography (e.g. 1994: 76-7), he nonetheless stressed the negative aspects of slave life most. Bradley's books are sometimes mistaken by students for textbooks. They are in fact polemics, reactions against historians (e.g. Kudlien in Chapter 2), who focussed on the 'success stories' of ancient slavery. Bradley argued that discipline, fear and insecurity, not humanity, best helped explain the survival of slavery for so long. Even when privileges were given to the slave, they were (deliberately) precarious. Slave family life was insecure, and most slaves lived in material poverty (see e.g. 1994: ch. 5 with 1984: ch. 2). They were often powerless, vulnerable to physical and sexual abuse.

Bradley therefore has a passionate commitment to noble aims. He allows us to imagine whole facets of Roman slave life that our sources hardly reported. I have no reason to challenge large parts of his findings. I will argue, however, that, as with our earlier case-studies, there are points in his description of slave life where he may be writing a story into the evidence rather than deducing one from it. This is perhaps clearest in two areas: his use of Roman law and comparative evidence.

Bradley, like most of the other authors we have been examining, was keen to stress the level of slave resistance, both passive and active (Bradley 1989). He argued that slaveowners were unable to see such resistance as anything other than selfish 'criminality' (1994: 122-3). Elite sources might suggest 'willing acquiescence' from slaves but (1994: 125):

Beneath the surface calm which elitist writings evince, however, there was a constant ferment of defiant activity as slaves, of every description, ran away, stole, cheated, damaged property and shirked work, or as they directed violence against themselves or their owners, all in an effort to withstand the cruelty and deprivation slavery heaped upon them. At no point in the central period of Roman history can it be said that passive acceptance of subjection was characteristic of the entire slave population.

One can only agree that 'passive acceptance' was not 'characteristic of the entire slave population', though that still leaves unclear what a 'constant ferment of defiant activity' might mean. An earlier passage of Bradley's might help explain. Roman legal writers, he noted, took it as read 'that slaves stole in all manner of circumstances' (1994: 116). A slave hired to work in a shop, for example, 'could be expected to steal' from those hiring them, slaves working on ships and inns might steal from freemen, a slave undertaker 'could be expected to steal' from corpses. He also gave a whole list of examples of slaves destroying property: 'the catalogue of slave crimes known to jurists was endless'. Those crimes could even involve slaves causing injury to themselves, for example pretending they had been hurt while defending a murdered master so as to prevent their own execution under the *senatus consultum Silanianum*. Literate slaves were able to harm masters by forgery or falsifying records. 'Tampering with records could become habitual', according to at least one legal source (Bradley 1994: 117). Bradley was able to give many more examples of ill-doing, with a whole series of references to Roman legal texts (notably the *Digest*). At first sight his position appears rock solid. There are, however, different ways in which his evidence *could* be read. Much of Roman law involves property rights. Damage caused by slaves could raise tricky problems, since slaves were themselves property. How far were the slaves themselves to be held responsible for what wrongs they did, and how far were their masters responsible? Who should make good any damage done, and in what way? Should the slaves be surrendered to the wronged party, or not? Romans lawyers had to be ready to answer such questions, so it is no surprise that Bradley should be able to cite examples. Crucially, however, such evidence need not necessarily imply anything as to the *commonness* of such crimes, apart from the fact that they could happen sometimes. It returns us to a problem similar to that we encountered in Chapter 2. In any particular case were jurists discussing a case because it was typical, or because it was possible, or because it was frankly unusual but raised academically interesting issues? Bradley treats Roman law as 'hard evidence' (Bradley 1994: 38, cf. 1994: 8). Yet discussions such as that noted in *Digest* 21.1.17.3 (should a slave running from a fire or a collapsing building be regarded as running away from his/ her master?) suggests that some examples might be part of a more pedantic, legalistic, debate. With this in mind, let us return to just a few of Bradley's examples.

(1) A hired slave, or a slave on a ship or an inn, or a slave working for an undertaker, for example, *could* be a thief, but nothing in the laws cited (*Digest* 19.2.45.pr-1, and 47.5.1.5, 4.9.3.3, 14.3.5.8), suggested that they 'could be expected' to be one. The main concern of these texts is how restitution should be made: was a 'noxal' action, with the surrender of

the slave to the injured party, enough? The texts may not be interested specifically in the free, but they imply that they too can be thieves (e.g. *Digest* 47.5.1.5), and they also contain discussions where slaves are not the perpetrators but the victims (*Digest* 19.2.42 discusses what happens if it is the hired slave that is stolen!). Finally, if slaves *might* deliberately damage property, the law discussed not only what should happen if they did this on their own initiative but also what should happen if they did so at the behest of their master (e.g. *Digest* 47.7.7.4).

(2) Slaves *might* cause physical damage to themselves, but, as Bradley noted, the '*senatus consultum Silanianum*' concerned those slaves due for execution when their master died in mysterious circumstances. The passage cited from the *Digest* (29.5.1.37) asked whether those who claimed to have been wounded while defending their masters should be exempted. Not, it answered, if they had wounded themselves to circumvent the law. Is this social reportage – or legalistic discussion?

(3) Slaves *might* tamper 'habitually' with records, but this *possibility* is mentioned in a discussion of the law on the corruption of slaves by a third party (*Digest* 11.3.11.1). Should someone who had induced a slave to tamper with financial records be responsible for all the future occasions the slave committed fraud solely for their own benefit? The answer given was no. Once again, it could be argued that the answer is designed to deal with a specific point of law rather than serve as a generalisation about slaves.

(4) Could a slave writing a will 'be expected' to indulge in forgery (*Digest* 48.10.22.9)? The passages cited from the

Digest only suggest, once more, that they might. Roman lawyers discussed forgery and falsehood by people of a range of different statuses, not just slaves (*Digest* 48.10 *passim*). It would indeed have been astonishing if slaves had not been included. It would have implied a belief by lawmakers that slaves were more honest than the free.

According to Bradley, however, Roman legal writers saw all slaves as 'corruptible beings' who could be persuaded to act in 'morally reprehensible ways' (1994: 123). They were regarded as prone to drunkenness and gambling and other vices. Their misbehaviour was due to their general characteristics of 'cunning' (*calliditas*) and effrontery. In sum the slave was, again according to Ulpian, '*onerosus*', a 'troublesome property'.

Once again Bradley's evidence can be read in a number of ways. To say, for example, that lawyers believed all slaves were *capable* of being corrupted is literally correct. Any slave might be corrupted. In just the same way, however, British law assumes that all men can be murderers: there are no individuals who, because of their status or position, *cannot* potentially be tried for murder. The ease with which we may be reading something into our evidence when we think we are reading something from it can be seen clearly in Bradley's discussion of '*calliditas*'. Two citations are offered (1994: 123n25). The first is *Digest* 15.3.3.9. If a man's slave claims to borrow money from a third party for his master and then uses it himself, the master has only limited liability for the theft. Otherwise the master would be injured unfairly by the 'credulity of the creditor' or the 'cunning [*calliditas*] of his

82

slave'. Clearly *calliditas* or plausibility need not be associated with slaves *in general* any more than gullibility is with creditors. There is no implication that slaves are expected to be frauds, but rather a technical discussion of a master's liability *if* a slave should behave fraudulently. The second citation is *Digest* 47.4.1.pr-1. A slave is promised freedom, but then a fraud he has committed is discovered. Should he escape punishment for the crime since he is technically between slavery and freedom? It would hardly be fair to let someone go unpunished in this situation, especially someone 'made bolder by the expectation' that he couldn't be charged (47.4.1.1):

> And so, because of this the praetor reckoned that the cunning and impudence of those who pillage inheritances should be curbed by a double legal action.

The reference to '*calliditatem*' can, again, hardly be associated *generically* with slaves. There are, in fact, several dozen uses of words with a '*callid*- root in the *Digest*. Only three (including the two cited) definitely refer to slaves. Most of the others could refer to either slave or free, with no reason to prefer either. A number refer definitely or very plausibly to the free (10.4.11.1, 11.3.3, 16.1.2.3, 17.1.6.7, 24.3.22.8, 49.4.1 pr). If one adopted a naive statistical approach, one could conclude that *calliditas* was something lawmakers associated mainly with *free* people. Why then might Bradley have made such a strong connection with slaves? Perhaps because the *servus callidus*, the cunning slave who cheats his master, is a major character in Roman comedy and Bradley is interpreting the legal evidence in that light. We shall see in the next chapter that even the apparently clear connection between slavery and 'cunning' in Roman comedy raises difficult problems of interpretation.

Bradley uses two other pieces of legal evidence to argue for a connection between slavery and criminality. *Digest* 21.18. pr does indeed show that 'any slave might be led to steal' etc., While, however, it illustrates a spectrum of possible slave behaviour, and while it certainly shows that slaves were corruptible, it tells us nothing as to whether this behaviour was typical. Finally, there is the *servus onerosus* or 'troublesome slave' we find in *Digest* 17.1.8.4. The original context, however, hardly supports any wider 'metaphorical' use of the passage. An orphan has a number of legal guardians. One guardian agrees with the others to buy a slave for the child but fails to do so. Who can sue whom? Should the other guardians sue the person who has not carried out his duty? Or can a case also be brought on behalf of the boy? Well, 'Julian draws a distinction'. Someone can sue on the boy's behalf only if the child has suffered a loss because he didn't have the slave. He cannot sue if the slave wasn't needed, if it was '*onerosus*'. While Alan Watson (like Bradley) translated *onerosus* as 'troublesome' it could, equally, mean 'burdensome, that is something bringing less benefit than it costs. Once again it need not have the kind of generic implications that Bradley implies it has.

Much of Bradley's concern in this section of his book was, admittedly, the inability of Roman slaveowners to read (principled) resistance to slavery among their slaves as being anything other than criminal behaviour and moral failure. He also suggested, however, that this material added up to a 'ferment' of opposition: how far it can be judged so from such texts is, however, open to doubt. This is not to suggest that slaves were passive, and there is certainly enough evidence to indicate that flight (for example) may have been common. It is difficult, however, to move from accepting the *possibility* of certain other actions (including suicide and murder) to assessing their frequency, even if it is clear they were considered very serious when they did they happen.

Bradley, however, felt that the legal sources were supported by other literary texts (1994: 123):

Pilfering could be forgiven if a slave had special gifts which endeared him to an owner, but the slave's tendency to commit wicked deeds was regarded, by Cicero (*Att.* 7.2.8) among others, as normal, so that when a newly manumitted slave betrayed the trust set in him, abandoned an important assignment and absconded, that was the unpardonable but typical behaviour of a reprobate that left Cicero no alternative but to revoke the grant of freedom. For Quintilian (*Inst.* 4.2.69), it was a given that slaves should always be trying to explain their shortcomings ('peccata'), an attitude like that of Cicero and countless others that was predicated on standards of undeviating obedience which slaveowners insisted upon from their slaves. When the standards were met, slaves were good; when not, they were bad.

Again, if the point of this passage is simply to show that

Romans had a concept of the 'bad' slave, one can agree. But if the behaviour of Chrysippus was 'normal', why did Cicero react with quite the fury clearly evident in his *Letter to Atticus* 7.2.8? Was it because it offended the 'standards of undeviating obedience' that Cicero (and others) *expected*?

I do not wish to be misunderstood, however. I am attempting to illustrate some of the steps in Bradley's argument, not argue their opposite. Roman lawyers had little reason to legislate on most forms of slave indiscipline. If a slave stole from his master, the master had no need of a lawyer or the *Digest* to deal with the problem: he had a whip. Roman writers generally had little incentive to emphasise slave resistance, and might have deliberately downplayed it. It may well be true, therefore, that the resistance we can see in our sources is merely the tip of the iceberg. We cannot tell.

The difficulties of using legal evidence are not just confined to our reading of the 'criminal' slave. Bradley used them also to suggest how precarious a slave's life might be. He discussed the powers of the city prefect, which included the hearing of complaints from starving slaves (1994: 100):

> How common or successful such complaints were it is impossible to tell. But they cannot all have been without foundation.

Bradley noted that cases were envisaged where slaves might starve because food was not delivered to the household or because food rotted or was destroyed by fire. Beside such accidents, however, there could be more deliberate action in times of crisis, as when gladiators and slaves on the market were expelled from Rome during a grain shortage. He concluded (1994: 101):

> Slaves who were unable to guarantee from day to day how or if they might adequately clothe and feed themselves might not always have shared the slaveowner's romantic view of the *familia* as a miniature state, a protective environment in which their wishes would be respected and implemented ....

Once more there is a distinction between what these statements say and what they imply. How many slaves lived in fear of starvation? The powers of the city prefect (*Digest* 1.12.1.8) reflected the possibility that masters might starve their slaves, but (a) they also, of course, reflected a desire by the state to do something about it and (b) such behaviour was associated in law with 'savagery', 'harshness' and obscenity. Slaves may regularly have received worse food than their masters, but was fear of starvation a significant element in their lives? While *Digest* 19.1.21.3, cited by Bradley, does indeed suggest that slaves might be accidentally starved when a shipment of food goes astray, the example was put forward to illustrate a legal principle: limited liability. The person responsible for the (non) delivery of the food can be sued only for the cost of the grain, not for further damage, *even if your slaves starve because of it*. Now the point may have been made because it was common or typical or possible. Or it could have been made because it stated a legal point in an unforgettable way. How does one decide between these interpretations? Finally, while one might imagine it only common sense that slaves should starve first in time of famine, it should be remembered that they were also pieces of property whose death could occasion serious financial loss (though Suetonius *Augustus* 42 does suggest that at least part of the servile population was sent away from Rome during a famine in the reign of the first emperor).

Bradley's particular reading of his evidence is also clear in his discussion of laws enacted to protect slaves. He is (generally) cynical both as to their motives and their effectiveness. Excesses were to prevented so as to secure peace and order among the slaves, to the benefit of the slaveholding class as a whole, not for humanitarian reasons (1984: 129):

> The arbitrary physical abuse of slaves cannot be said to have been dramatically alleviated by legislation of an improving kind.

It could be argued, however, that there is a tension between arguing that the laws were both ineffective and enacted only for cynical reasons.. If the laws were ineffective, how could they have worked to relieve tensions and act as a safety valve? One *could* indeed argue that the very cynicism Bradley ascribed to the Roman legislation is the best argument we have in favour of its potential effectiveness. I have actually no brief to argue in favour of one side or the other of this debate. I simply wish to show the difficulties of dealing with this material. Bradley, however, argued that the 'impression' given by 'anecdotal and random evidence' is that legal changes were likely to have had 'no more than a small impact on slave life' (1994: 171-2). He quoted a case from an Egyptian papyrus

(P.Oxy. 903) to illustrate the vulnerability of slaves to 'capricious brutality' and the difficulty in using 'mechanisms of relief'. A wife complains about her husband:

> He shut up his own slaves and mine with my foster-daughters and his agent and son for seven whole days in his cellars, having insulted his slaves and my slave Zoë and half-killed them with blows, and he applied fire to my foster-daughters, having stripped them quite naked, which is contrary to the laws ... and to the slaves when they were being beaten he said, 'What did she [i.e. his wife] take from my house?' and they under torture said, 'She has taken nothing of yours, but all your property is safe.'

Here are the conclusions Bradley drew:

> In this example distinctions of status obviously had no bearing on the way the husband behaved; his victims were not slaves alone. But in dealing with his suspicions that his wife had stolen from him, the husband was clearly not deterred by Roman imperial legislation from interrogating, battering and incarcerating the slaves of his household as much as he wished, and to the slaves the theoretical rights of appeal to the provincial governor and taking refuge before a statue of the emperor were, in the heat of crisis, useless.

This material can indeed be used to support Bradley's case, but, once again, it can be read in a different fashion. One might argue that the wife feels that the abuse of the slaves is as worthy of inclusion in her plea (and apparently as shocking) as the abuse of the free. Nothing in the story implies that her primary concern is simply damage to her property. Secondly, if her husband was undeterred by the law, criminals have always broken the law, even in modern society. Bradley himself remarked that the violence here was directed at both slave *and free*: should we therefore deduce that the laws against assault of the free were meaningless in the Roman empire? Even if the slaves had not managed to avail themselves of asylum (is that point relevant given the nature of the attack?), the whole story *could* be cited to illustrate an expectation that the state would be concerned with their mistreatment, in contrast to Bradley's emphasis. One's overall argument can determine one's reading of particular texts.

It could be argued, indeed, that Bradley may have been over-estimating the importance of legislation, and underestimating that of social attitudes, returning us to points discussed with reference to Garrido-Hory and Shtaerman and Trofimova in Chapters 2 and 3. In his 1984 book Bradley recalled some stories of sadism from the early Roman empire from authors such as Juvenal and Seneca (1984: 121-2). He accepted that many of these stories survived because they were regarded as extreme examples of cruelty, but argued that they showed that there was 'no real restraint' on the behaviour of slave owners other than their own 'temperament or conscience' (122). Punishment of slave misbehaviour was likely to be very harsh. Now, while Bradley was certainly correct that there was little *legal* protection in the early empire, was there 'no real restraint on the slave-owner'? I suggested earlier that the stories from authors such as Juvenal and Seneca may themselves have operated as a restraint. While we might see public opinion as a particularly imperfect mechanism of social control and prefer legislative action, we should not assume the same for Romans (see e.g. Seneca, *On Mercy* 1.22.2-1.23.2). Unwarranted cruelty was bad form. Why do authors such as Cicero or the Younger Pliny seek to portray themselves (like many others represented in inscriptions) as being good to 'their people'? There could still be a very wide definition of what constituted 'warranted' cruelty. Extreme cruelty was certainly not prevented. But, as discussed earlier, if we cite Juvenal or Martial or Seneca *only* for examples of cruelty, we are missing another aspect of Roman slavery, the fact that there was obviously some debate about the limits of ill-treatment. Discussion of the creation of such 'norms' of behaviour was not, however, part of Bradley's project, and his reader needs to realise that.

Roman legal and literary evidence therefore provides the historian with both opportunities and problems. The very difficulty in pinning the material down allows it to be used in a variety of ways. The same is also true of the comparative evidence (from modern Atlantic slave societies) that Bradley uses to try to get inside the 'psychological world' of the Roman slave. Bradley recognised some 'traditional' complaints about the use of such material but argued that it would be 'arrogant' to believe that the classical world was unique (1994: 180):

Modern historians and sociologists, knowing full well the need to make every allowance for particular variations in one society after another, have disclosed nonetheless the universalist features of slavery across time and place: to pretend otherwise is futile.

If the key features of slave systems were 'universal' one might ask why historians should actually bother to study those, like Rome's, with comparatively little evidence. The difficulty, of course, is in deciding precisely *which* features are common between different slave societies. Any survey of the scholarship on modern slave societies will quickly make clear the lack of agreement. Particular areas have seen a succession of widely different interpretations (compare the different views on US slavery famously developed during the course of the twentieth century by Ulrich Phillips (1929), Kenneth Stampp (1956) and Eugene Genovese (1974)). Historians of slavery in Africa (for example) have sometimes stressed the 'integration' of slaves into society much more than their counterparts working on slavery in the 'New World' (see e.g. Miers and Kopytoff 1977; Fisher 2001). Slave systems can differ along a number of axes (e.g. the importance of racial differences or of the extent to which there is a perceived need to maximise profit), and the issue then becomes how far those factors might impact on other features of slavery. How different, then, might various *slaveries* be? How, precisely, do we 'make ... allowance for individual variations'?

Let us examine an example of the difficulties involved. In his 1984 book Bradley discussed the precariousness of slave life and wondered what impact this may have had upon slave psychology (1984: 142):

4. Keith Bradley: Passionate about Slavery

Since no accounts written by slaves of their experiences during slavery exist, the extent of this posited emotional factor in servile life cannot be adequately evaluated. It is not capable of measurement. But some support is available in the form of analogy, even though analogy cannot be used as absolute proof in and of itself for the generally bleak conditions of Roman slaves which have been suggested.

He argued that the 'coercive power' of slaveowners might have created 'submissive', even childlike behaviour among slaves. He cited research by US scholars on the compliant 'Sambo' characterisation of slaves by US slaveowners. Bradley himself mentioned that there had been 'intense debate' over this issue. The last twenty years have seen the mainstream of research in the US move away from such positions. The emphasis has been much more on slave resistance and, in the words of the subtitle to Eugene Genovese's ground-breaking 1974 book *Roll Jordan, Roll*: 'The world the slaves made'. It may be significant that Bradley's 1994 monograph made much less of slave acquiescence. Our picture of the US slave of the mid-nineteenth century was changing in the later part of the twentieth, and Bradley's arguments reflect that change. The debate among US scholars does not in any way invalidate Bradley's position if one views comparative evidence as expanding the range of potential views and ideas, helping our imagination. Bradley, after all, suggested only that this material 'may' help us salvage the experience of the slave. If, however, we feel that US material helps fill gaps in the Roman record, this kind of disagreement becomes much more problematic.

It should be no surprise also that modern US material can be just as difficult to interpret as ancient Roman. Bradley illustrates this himself. He wondered what Roman slaves thought about their low standard of living. He turned for inspiration to the interviews with former US slaves made in the 1930s by the Works Progress Administration (Bradley 1994: 93-4). They showed (unsurprisingly) little fondness for the days of slavery before the Civil War (1861-5). There were some exceptions, however. Some contrasted their poor material conditions in the 1930s with those during slavery. Here is Bradley's response (1994: 94n21):

> Such recollections may have been affected by fading memories when the WPA interviews were taken or by the contemporary conditions of the Depression. They were not common to all.

Bradley himself noted that some historians have argued that some US and Brazilian slaves may have had better diets than some free European workers of the same period (94-5):

> But for immediate purposes, what needs to be stressed is that from their own perspective many slaves, whether well-fed, well-clothed, well-housed or not, were very much aware of the gulf that separated them from their owners and, more importantly, were equally aware of how their material dependence kept them anxiety-ridden and subject to their owners' control.

4. Keith Bradley: Passionate about Slavery

The US material allows us to imagine a situation where slaves deeply resented their material conditions, but Bradley himself has shown that the evidence can be contradictory. He explained away the (isolated?) evidence of more positive feelings. I have no wish to argue that US slaves were happy with their lot, but why question only one interpretation of the modern evidence in this manner? Some views of slavery in the WPA interviews may have actually been hardened by the political and social repression of the post-Civil War period. How far should we rely on them to represent the realities of seventy-five years previously? The solution, as Bradley in principle argued, is to read the US material as thought-provoking, but not to rely on it (even implicitly) to prove points about Roman society. One might indeed complain that this often condemns Roman slaves to silence. Is accepting the problems with this kind of evidence, however, better or worse than potentially putting *our* words in their mouths?

No historian has tried harder than Bradley to restore the voice of ancient slaves and rescue them from anonymity. None has tried harder to give a hint of the potential misery lying behind the complacency and snobbery of the literary sources. He is one of the very few authors who have offered a global survey of the life of the Roman slave. If that survey emphasised mainly the harshest aspects of a slave's life, one cannot claim Bradley has not warned his reader of his aims, and he *may* be quite correct in his emphasis. His work, however, constitutes a polemic, albeit a polemic with an enemy who (certainly for most Anglophone readers) remains hidden: the approach suggested by some of those connected with the Mainz *Forschungen* who are sometimes perhaps (too) ready to emphasise the 'positives' in the lives of slaves. Bradley's moral beliefs, particularly his hatred of cruelty and oppression, are clear in his work, and form a great part of its strength. I have tried, however, to show how this has sometimes affected his reconstruction of Roman slavery, leading him, like the other authors we have studied, to favour particular interpretations where the evidence often remains ambiguous.

'I too want to tell a story ...': Some Modern Literary Scholars and Ancient Slavery

The title of this chapter comes from an article by Keith Hopkins, a specialist on ancient social history notable for his capacity to anticipate new directions in the field (Hopkins 1993: 10). By the early 1990s he was expressing unease with some of the kinds of approaches we have discussed in previous chapters. He noted the difficulty of producing history from anecdotes, such as the story of Vedius Pollio's attempt, discussed above, to feed a slave to his lampreys for breaking a goblet (1993: 4ff., esp. 8-9). The story can be cited to show what a Roman slaveowner was capable of doing to his slaves, but it also illustrates that others found this unacceptable. Hopkins regarded such stories as the means by which Romans thought about extremes rather than as 'typical' examples of their behaviour. He was keen, nonetheless, to stress that Roman sources showed that vicious punishment of slaves was quite permissible. Crucially, however, Hopkins argued that historians should not just add up historical examples of good or bad treatment (the 'anecdotal' approach). They should investigate how Roman writers *thought* about slavery and how they expected their audience to respond to their stories. This offered an escape from the problems of generalising from particular examples and paid greater heed to the aims of individual ancient authors. The failure to do this produced many of the problems with the 'global' interpretations of slavery discussed in the previous chapters.

The classicist William Fitzgerald published a short book surveying a series of analyses which mirrored Hopkins' new approach (Fitzgerald 2000). Keith Bradley, some of whose work we discussed in the last chapter, was scathing in response (Bradley 2001). Their disagreement goes to the heart of the debate about the reconstruction of Roman slavery. Bradley felt that Fitzgerald was toying with dangerous ideas that a degree of 'humanity' somehow existed in ancient slavery, possibly because Fitzgerald was willing to discuss material from epitaphs and poetry suggesting emotional bonds between master and slave (Bradley 2001: 475). Secondly, Bradley felt Fitzgerald represented a 'postmodernist party line' which believed it was somehow possible, after the passage of several millennia, to trace 'anxieties' about slaves within the psyche of the Roman slaveowner (Bradley 2001: 476). Bradley argued that Fitzgerald detached individual literary sources so much from their original historical context that the interpretations offered often said more about the modern writer than the ancient world. There was 'hard' evidence on ancient slavery which contradicted the occasional stories of intimacy from the 'soft' imaginative literature: e.g. slave chains and direct statements of tensions from Roman historians and politicians (ibid.). When Bradley suggested that

5. 'I too want to tell a story ...'

Fitzgerald had produced a book more welcome to literary scholars than to historians, this was not meant as a compliment (Bradley 2001: 477). We shall return to the distinction later.

Bradley has a point in querying some of Fitzgerald's interpretations, particularly those that delve into the psychological world of Roman slaveowners. Nineteenth-century concepts used by Fitzgerald, such as 'castration complexes' or 'labour alienation', may indeed help us understand ancient slavery, irrespective of whether the Romans themselves explicitly understood such ideas. The problem, however, is that Fitzgerald attempts to generalise from isolated pieces of evidence such as Martial, *Epigrams* 11.58 and Horace, *Odes* 1.38 (Fitzgerald 2000: 47-50 and 27-31, with Fitzgerald 1989). The smaller the evidential base, however, the greater the danger of reading modern ideas *into* such texts, rather than *from* them. The Martial passage (supposedly illustrating a fear of castration by one's slaves) concerns the slave barber we met in our discussion of Garrido-Hory's work in Chapter 2. We saw there the difficulty of generalising from this text. It would be comforting to think that Roman slaveowners suffered existential and psychoanalytical crises because of slavery, but while we *can* use Martial or Horace to suggest this, there seems little to support the idea that we *should*. Psychoanalysing living people can be difficult enough – psychoanalysing those dead for two millennia is even more so.

Fitzgerald does, indeed, also seem at other times to offer a fairly positive view of relations between masters and owners (see, e.g., 2000: 4-5, 14-16, 36, 54). He did recognise, however, that the bulk of our evidence comes from the slaveowners and that it concentrates on the relatively privileged urban and domestic slaves (2). As if to try to balance this, Fitzgerald finished his book with a passage showing striking similarities to Bradley's own work, citing evidence from modern American slavery to help us imagine the indignities of slavery from the viewpoint of the slave (118).

Whether or not Fitzgerald held a 'positive' view of ancient slavery, his overall approach still has the potential to undermine Bradley's more negative view. Fitzgerald showed just how sophisticated our reading of the ancient evidence might need to be, how many literary and intellectual cross-currents may affect how it was written. Romans were, after all, not famous English actors in togas (or, for that matter, US plantation owners speaking Latin), but people living in an alien culture whose nuances can be opaque to us. Let us take the example of Horace's *Satires* 2.7 (Fitzgerald 2000: 18-24, cf. Highet 1973: 272-6; Muecke 1993: 83-9; Oliensis 1998: 52ff.). It is not important in itself: it simply illustrates how complex interpretation can be. Horace is at home. One of Horace's slaves, Davus, unexpectedly speaks out. Even more unexpectedly he proceeds to criticise his master at length: Horace is not leading a life appropriate to a true gentleman. What does the episode tell us about relations between master and slave? Should we see this as an example of intimacy within a slave household, where a slave can lecture his master? Or should we rather note Horace's evident surprise and his threat to send Davus off to work on the farm (*Satires* 2.7.118)? Should we instead concentrate on the name of the slave (Davus), and the insults directed against him (e.g. *furcifer*, *Satires* 2.7.22), both of which are oddly reminiscent of the world of Greek and Roman comic plays? Are these signs to the audience that the whole thing is meant as a huge joke? Or should we read events within a 'Saturnalian' context, where masters and slaves swap places for a day (*Satires* 2.7.4-5)? Perhaps, instead, Davus represents not a slave but the silent (free) audience who have been listening (im)patiently to Horace's hypocritical moralising in the rest of the *Satires*? After all, undermining one's moral authority, playing with the persona of the poet could all be part of the poetic game. Someone needs to take the author down a peg: a slave would be an ironic choice. Or could Davus' intervention have been read as Horace's self-mocking commentary on the 'enslavement' of poet to patron in Rome (if Horace lowered himself to the position of slave in taking presents from his wealthy patrons why *shouldn't* a slave talk back to him?). Could the exchange be meant as a humorous reference to the fashionable Stoic idea that the morally good man is free and the bad man a slave whatever their legal status? Then Davus would have as much right to speak as Horace! Finally, might Horace's bad-tempered response to Davus be related to his own shame at his own father's slave origins and desire to distance himself from them (cf. Highet 1973; Williams 1995)? Perhaps different elements of these interpretation should be mixed together, but we are still left with the (irresolvable) question of which elements and in what proportions. We have seen that Bradley had an emotional commitment to rescuing the real slave from the silence of the slaveowning sources. Here the 'real' slave starts to disappear entirely, to be replaced by the 'imaginary' slave through whom slaveowners think about aspects of their *own* existence. This kind of approach poses real problems for social historians.

We saw that Bradley argued that there was 'hard' evidence with which one might compare Fitzgerald's 'soft' evidence. We have, however, seen in earlier chapters some of the difficulties with the 'hard' evidence (including Roman law, or the *Letters* of Pliny). This is not to suggest that reading stories in technical or historical texts throws up exactly the same kinds of problems (or, even, arguably, as many) as reading poetry, but that each produces their own. More than thirty years ago René Martin brilliantly showed how the works of Roman agricultural writers such as Varro and Columella may have been affected by earlier poetic and philosophical traditions (Martin 1971). To give another instance, the historian Tacitus also cannot be isolated from the imaginative world. For example, in his *Annals* (14.39), he described how an imperial freedman (an ex-slave) was sent by the emperor Nero to check on the behaviour of a governor of the newly conquered province of Britain. We might expect Tacitus, as a Roman aristocrat, to have been angered by this. More interesting, however, is the alleged reaction of the Britons. Tacitus tells us that they too were astonished that a Roman general should be ordered around by a slave. It is just about possible, one supposes, that the Britons were indeed aware of the internal politics of the event, or cared about them. But when one finds Tacitus detailing the (surely secret) negotiations among some of the emperor Claudius' freedmen to determine who should be the new empress (*Annals* 12.1-3), one wonders whether we are reading about what was going on inside the imperial court or inside Tacitus' mind. Was someone keeping minutes? Even archaeological evidence has its problems. Bradley cites Thompson's work on slave chains as 'hard' evidence of the way Romans treated their slaves (Bradley 2001: 475n3, Thompson 1993). Thompson's work, however, indicated that the bulk of surviving manacles and fetters from the Roman period come from the edges of the empire, often from river deposits. This *might* tell us something about the treatment of captives, but little about the treatment of domestic slaves within the empire. All this, of course, leads us right back into the 'soft' imaginative texts we were trying to escape. The 'hard' evidence can be just as 'self-deconstructing' as that examined by Fitzgerald and the other authors we shall meet in this chapter.

I noted, however, that Fitzgerald's book actually doesn't pose much of an *explicit* challenge to Bradley's work. Ironically, this is at least partly because Fitzgerald did not develop a postmodern party line. While Fitzgerald discussed 'overdetermination', that is to say the existence of multiple meanings for literary texts (2000: 10), he did not explore what this might do to our overall interpretation of the evidence on slavery (as opposed to its effect on the discussion of individual pieces of evidence). He did not attempt to undermine traditional narratives. Indeed, with regard to 'castration complexes' or 'labour alienation' he was happy to ascribe meaning where social historians would probably be more cautious. Bradley is, nevertheless, correct that Fitzgerald's potential 'opening up' of interpretation is more likely to suit those trained as classicists rather than historians. Classicists enjoy exploring extra 'meanings' of a text. Historians, however, usually prefer to narrow down interpretations and present a single picture. The problem for an historian like Bradley may come not when Fitzgerald does 'bad' history but when he does 'good' classics. This illustrates a division in the study of ancient slavery going beyond those seen earlier in this book (e.g. the changes over time seen in Chapter 1 or the geographical/ political divisions seen in Chapters 2-5).

Paradoxically, Fitzgerald's 'party line' has, therefore, little to do with postmodernism. His training as a classicist might lead him to produce multiple readings of ancient slavery. He limits them, however, as do many of the other classicists we shall meet in this chapter, by unconsciously accepting a 'background' for their interpretations offered by 'textbooks' such as Bradley's. This gives them a 'context' within which to interpret their literary material.

Bradley was correct, however, that many literary scholars want to see 'anxieties' in the relationship between master and slave (though this book has tried to show that this desire is shared by many historians too). These 'anxieties' are usually seen as founded on the 'contradiction' between the slave as a piece of property, an object, and the slave as subject, a human being who could affect his or her surroundings and impinge on the life of his or her master. Kathleen McCarthy's work on the slave in Roman love poetry has been one of the subtlest of the investigations into this 'contradiction' (McCarthy 1998). She observed that Roman poets sometimes imagined themselves as the slave of their beloved or a slave of love itself (e.g. Tibullus 2.4.1-6, Propertius 1.9.19-30: McCarthy focuses on Ovid, *Amores* 1.3, *Art of Love* 2.339-72, Propertius 1.1.27-28). The metaphor could be interpreted either as masochistic or as deliberately ironic. McCarthy, however, argued that it also reflected Romans' fear of their slaves. They wanted slaves to be capable agents and intermediaries, able at times to think for themselves. On the other hand, they realised that they never quite knew what their slaves were thinking and whether they could be trusted. The very skills masters might look for in a slave could be used by the slave against them. Masters were also dependent upon their slaves for many of their basic physical needs. The idea of the lover as slave, worming his way into the life of his mistress, played on the fears this could create (McCarthy 1998: esp. 178-80).

McCarthy doesn't just argue from the poems themselves, but cites what she sees as supporting evidence that Romans had anxieties about the control of their slaves (1998: 181-2). I will argue in detail later in this chapter that some of that evidence, for example the comic plays of Plautus or the *Life of Aesop*, need not imply such unease. Her remaining evidence is also problematic. Pliny the Elder certainly expressed a fear of slave doctors (*Natural Histories* 29.7), but we have already noted that most Romans continued to trust them. The philosopher Seneca certainly castigated some masters for the extent of their material and intellectual dependence upon their slaves and servants (*Letters to Lucilius* 27.5-8). Given, however, his (Stoic) belief that proper gentlemen should live independently, he may have exaggerated the degree of dependence to make his point more forceful. Few owners seem actually to have divested themselves of their useful (human) tools. Finally, Petronius' *Satyricon* portrays the rich freedman Trimalchio as both dependent upon, and over-attached to, his slaves. He even brings them in to eat dinner with his guests (*Satyricon* 74). Trimalchio is, however, a character designed to look ludicrous in a whole series of ways (from his toilet habits to his ignorant mangling of mythology: *Satyricon* 27 and 48). Rather than representing a wide-spread 'fear', one could argue instead that dependence upon one's slaves was a sign of deviance and weakness (cf. the attacks made upon the emperor Claudius for over-dependence upon women and freedmen, most famously expressed in the *Apolocyntosis* or *'Pumpkinification of Claudius'*). All these pieces of evidence *can* then be cited by McCarthy to provide a 'context' for her views on the use of the metaphor of the 'poet-as-slave', but they can also be interpreted in a manner that is less helpful to her. Do they show a basic fear of Roman slaveowners, or an outlandish possibility afflicting only the feckless? If one wanted, one could avoid this dilemma by arguing that Petronius and others are 'repressing' their fear, portraying dependence upon slaves as something affecting only the feckless because of a desire to reassure their audience and allay their own worries. But how would one prove such a view? It could be either (a) a highly useful theory corresponding to reality or (b) a rhetorical device designed to dismiss awkward evidence. The problem is judging which is more likely to be the case.

Even if one accepts the contextual material, there are difficulties with McCarthy's interpretation of the lover-as-slave. If the lover can (potentially) use his position to his advantage, how far is that because he is (in the eyes of the audience if not in the logic of the poem) both slave *and* poet (see McCarthy 1998: 179)? He is a 'slave' with all the wiles of the aristocratic author. If he is read by the audience as an example of what a poet could do *were he in the position of the slave*, it need not say much of what those Romans thought (or feared) about ordinary slaves. McCarthy also admits that the poet slave is never allowed to 'win' in the poems (1998: 182). He *cannot* be seen to win, she suggests, an example of a 'repression of fear' argument. It remains, however, just as easy (easier?) to argue the slave image was chosen not because of its 'power' but because of the humiliation involved and the images of torture and pain which McCarthy herself recognises in the poems (177). This makes the persona of the poet-slave all the more exciting and paradoxical *as a literary artifice*. Romans *may* have feared the 'power' given to their slaves. As we shall discuss further below, power can indeed be a reciprocal relationship, to a certain extent. It is difficult, however, to argue that point convincingly from these poems. McCarthy could be right, but the evidence equally allows her to be wrong. She raises a fascinating possibility, *if* one believes the views of some of the authors examined in earlier chapters that masters lived in fear of slave resistance.

Hopkins' 1993 work on the (fictitious) biography of Aesop provides another example of the problem. Aesop, the writer of fables and slave of a philosopher, obeys his master's orders literally. This ensures that his master *never* gets what he wants (e.g. *Life of Aesop G* 38, Perry 1952: 49). For Hopkins the story (again) illustrated a tension in the mind of Roman slaveowners between wanting slaves to be passive tools but also useful (and therefore potentially independently-minded) agents (1993: 14). Hopkins was surely right not to dismiss the text merely as comedy: jokes may tell us much about a society.

There are, however, two difficulties with his approach. Firstly, can the events of the tale be explained without a 'fear' of slaves? Aesop's cleverness (and ugliness: *Life of Aesop G* 1, Perry 1952: 35) may refer to the never-never land of the 'clever slave' in Roman comedies (on the implications of these characters, see below). The fact that Aesop's master Xanthus is a philosopher may also be important (see Fitzgerald 2000: 34). The pompous intellectual has the slave he deserves and gets his just deserts and full humiliation from the lowest of the low. Aesop might, finally, also represent the philosopher Socrates, famous for guying those who felt they knew better than others. He, like Aesop, came to a violent end (as Hopkins himself noted, 1993: 25).

Hopkins, like McCarthy, attempts to provide some supporting evidence for his own interpretation. He notes that Plutarch (*Concerning Talkativeness* 18 = 511 DE) has a similar story about an overly literal slave (1993: 20n31):

> The story has the same point, or so it seems, as this section of the *Life of Aesop*: that is reassuring. What the *Life of Aesop* tells us is not so much new, as paralleled in its richness and its perspective.

This raises the interesting philosophical question of how many citations are required to make a context. One? Two? There is a danger of Hopkins falling back into the kind of 'anecdotal' history he was trying to escape. Hopkins' position seems no more secure than McCarthy's.

No genre has encouraged greater debate over Roman slaveowners' 'anxieties' than the comic plays of Plautus, which I have alluded to several times. I have inferred that there are difficulties in deciding what comic slaves may tell us about real slaves. It is time to explain why.

Roman comedies are often versions of much older plays produced in Greece. In the plays slaves often take control of the action (most famously in Plautus' *Pseudolus*). They generally help the young man of their household gain his (current) true love. This usually involves making a fool of the boy's father (the slave's master), and also humiliating undesirables such as pimps or mercenaries.

Some scholars have used evidence from the plays to argue for an optimistic reading of the relationship between masters and slaves. Joseph Vogt believed that Plautus showed bonds of trust between free and slave (1974: 131). He particularly stressed speeches in the plays where slaves expressed their keenness to do what their master wanted, even when he was absent (e.g. *Pseudolus* 1103ff., *The Rope* 914ff., *The Two Menaechmuses* 966ff.). There is an immediate problem with this. It is something of a leap of faith to believe that these speeches actually represent what slaves really thought. One could argue, of course, that they represent what the audience *believed*, or wanted to believe, slaves thought. Difficulties remain, however, given both the content of the speeches and their context. Many stress that the ultimate basis of obedience is the threat of violence. Secondly, as Richard Hunter demonstrated, these 'loyal slaves' quickly turn out to be fools who bungle their masters' affairs (Hunter 1985: 145-7). Even as they speak of their loyalty a (metaphorical) custard pie is arcing through the air to hit them in the face: irony is king.

Vogt's generally optimistic view of the plays was shared by

Jean Christian Dumont (1987: 307ff.). Comedy may have been a lie or fiction, but it could not have convinced its audience if it didn't reflect aspects of the truth (483ff., esp. 485, 488). It helps show how slavery was lived (311-12). Like Vogt, Dumont believed that the 'loyal slave' speeches constituted valuable evidence, though he argued that one should trust the sentiments of those delivered only when the master was absent from the stage (445, cf. 336, 603). The threat of violence was ever-present in the texts (401-2), but Dumont argued that there were plenty of incentives alongside the threats (402ff.). Slaves were not just 'speaking tools' (496n1256). The domestic slaves portrayed in the plays had the chance of a family life (even a form of marriage: 409-17), and access to pocket money which opened the road to freedom (418-34). Slavery was a temporary status (433). It could even be seen as an apprenticeship (592-3). Plautus portrays masters preparing for the integration of slaves into society through moral and decent (albeit self-interested) treatment (606). Sexual relationships between master and slave were not just the product of force and could cut through the slave/ free divide (333-4). Plautus' *The Captives* showed that the Romans were unwilling to accept earlier Greek ideas of a clear 'natural' distinction between free and slave (Dumont 1987: 588-93 and cf. Dumont 1974). In that play the 'good' slave Tyndarus is prepared to sacrifice himself to secure the freedom of his captured master: he is as noble as his master, if not more so.

One can only agree with Dumont that there is *some* reflection of social reality in the plays, but the difficulty is establishing precisely how much and where. The treatment of

110

the 'loyal slave' speeches is a case in point. Does the absence of a fictional master from the stage really give added truthfulness to the words of a stage slave? As another example of the problem, the commonness of some of the slave privileges claimed by Dumont (particularly manumission) is rather more difficult to establish than he implied. The idea that some form of pseudo-marriage existed for slaves in Rome faces a quite fundamental problem: the prologue of the play *Casina* expresses surprise at this idea (*Casina* 67ff.). Dumont argued that this statement was a latter addition to Plautus' text. Even if it was, however, whoever wrote it expected the audience to agree with it. As a final example, if Tyndarus in the *The Captives* is a 'noble' slave, we learn quite quickly that he was free-born (*The Captives* 8-10), and he eventually rejoins his family (1010ff.). His place as slave is taken by the evil runaway Stalagmus who fits quite neatly with the idea that some people deserved to be slaves. One could argue (with Thalmann, below) that Plautus actually reinforced the slave/ free distinction in the *Captivi* rather than undermined it.

Peter Spranger published a study of Roman comic slaves as part of the Mainz *Forschungen* (on which see Chapter 2). Like Dumont and Vogt, he took a fairly positive picture of slave/ master relations from the plays. He noted there were few overt signs of any unified resistance from slaves (1984: 32-5, though one might ask how many such signs we should expect in comedies). He argued that many elements of the plays had their roots in Greek rather than Roman society (63). Some elements, such as the scheming 'cunning' slave were, he felt, totally unbelievable in a Roman context (39ff., cf. 57ff.). Others, such as the listing of slaves as property, were common to both Greece and Rome (64ff.). Plautus, he suggested, was readier to portray threats of violence against slaves than his Greek predecessors (47ff.). Spranger believed that this illustrated the strength of the ideological divide in Rome between slave and free (86). On the other hand he argued that those making threats against slaves were often depicted as hotheads (48). He doubted whether it was possible to judge how common violence was in reality (48-9) and argued that some of the more extreme threats were likely to be unreal. Curiously he judged this from the fact that slaves on stage paid little heed to the threats (but why should *stage* slaves do so?), and from the alleged improbability of Romans of Plautus' time burning slaves out of places of asylum (surely something of a circular argument).

Most recent scholarship on the slave in Roman comedy has taken a different direction from Vogt, Dumont and Spranger. The approach was pioneered by authors such as Eric Segal (1987) and David Konstan (1983). They stressed the festival context in which the plays were produced. They drew on the medieval idea of *carnivale*: a festival time when it was permitted to depict the world turned upside down and to poke fun at one's social superiors. They saw the 'clever slave' as a tool to humiliate the rich, the powerful, the father-figure. Why choose a slave? Perhaps their very lowliness helped intensify the humiliation. Perhaps their so-called 'liminal' position, being able to view the action within households without being fully part of it, also made them attractive (cf. Bettini 1991). Perhaps they allowed the young to enjoy a vicarious victory over their elders without appearing to challenge the existing social structure too openly (Parker

1989). Fitzgerald raised the additional possibility that physical threats to slaves may have served to displace the anxieties felt by the audience about the vulnerability of their *own* bodies (2000: 39). This view was brusquely dismissed by Bradley (2001: 476): he had no wish to argue away evidence of violence against slaves.

Some recent literary and psychological readings do, however, attempt to bring the debate back to 'real' slavery, albeit indirectly. Holt Parker, not content with supplying one important new reading of Plautus' slaves, produced a second in the same seminal article in 1989. He argued that the cunning slave represented not only the 'young man' rebelling against the older generation, but also mirrored the fears raised by recent slave rebellions (see e.g. Livy 32.26, 33.36). The cunning slave allowed Romans to raise the spectre of difficult, rebellious slaves only to exorcise it by laughing at it. This is a possible reading, but there are difficulties. There seems no doubt that there were some slave risings at this time, but how far can we establish the level of fear they produced among owners? There is little contemporary evidence aside from the writings of Cato the Elder. We are largely left with Plautus himself. Since Parker was arguing that Plautus repressed the fear, we cannot expect much direct evidence there (curiously, Terence, writing comedies very shortly after Plautus, stressed the cunning slave much less). Parker's reading therefore remains a fascinating possibility, but there remain difficulties in finding evidence for it. In addition, Parker, in just one article, had produced *two* perfectly good reasons why slaves should be important in the plays, an example of what William Fitzgerald called the 'overdetermination' of meaning in literary texts. The plays apparently allowed the young to 'rebel' and *also* dealt with fears of slave rebellion. This could be either a welcome subtlety in interpretation or it could indicate how easy it is to create 'meanings' in a text.

Greg Thalmann warned against trying to discover 'the practices of slavery as an historical institution' from the comedy of Plautus (1996: 137). He argued, nonetheless, that we could discover something of how Roman slaveowners viewed their world. In a sense he offers a hope of bridging a little of the distance between some of the Mainz and Marxist approaches we examined in Chapters 2 and 3. He argued that slavery was an antagonistic, conflict-based social phenomenon, but that 'ideology' (representing the class interests of the slaveowners) operated to reinforce it and helped to explain its longevity. He focused on the play *The Captives*. The pairing of the 'noble' slave Tyndarus and 'bad' slave Stalagmus (mentioned above) ultimately offered a reassuring picture to the Romans. Two views of slavery were being offered. One was benevolent: the 'noble' slave suggested that masters could rely on the loyalty of their slaves. The other view of slavery was suspicious: the 'bad' slave suggested slavery was nonetheless natural and justified: such people had to be controlled and deserved their lot. Thalmann accepted that (117):

> these two models of slavery are at root incompatible with each other, and the contradiction between them reproduces the contradiction at the heart of slavery itself.

There is, of course, every reason to accept that literary texts

114

(and social ideas) can be contradictory, but this particular contradiction produces real difficulties for Thalmann's interpretation. How reassuring a symbol of slave loyalty *is* Tyndarus, given that his 'free' origins are highlighted from the start of the play? To what extent would the audience identify him with their own slaves? Further, did the sins of Stalagmus, kidnapper and scoundrel, really justify slavery for others? Or are both situated in what the audience would have seen clearly as a never-never world, operating as opposites to one another but with little connection to slave-owning as experienced outside the theatre?

Kathleen McCarthy, like Thalmann, has recently taken the debate away from the reading of just the 'cunning slave' in Plautus. She argued that plays such as *Casina* and *The Two Menaechmuses* illustrate the contradiction owners felt between their (theoretically) absolute power and the negotiations they had to engage in with their slaves in practice, promising freedom, etc. (McCarthy 2000: chs 2-3). In *Casina* Lysidamus, the master of the house, develops a crush on a servant-girl about to be married off to another slave within his household. The action revolves around his attempts to maintain sexual access to the girl. The more he tries to get his way, the more control he loses over his wife and his slaves, eventually being treated like a slave himself (*Casina* 937ff.). It could be argued, as McCarthy suggests, that the play shows the difficulties of exercising power within the household. But does the audience of slaveowners identify with Lysidamus' self-induced disasters? Or do they howl with laughter at a lunatic world where everything is turned on its head? What should we make of the fact that the slaves never act independently against Lysidamus but are led by his wife? Could the audience not imagine independent action by slaves, was it therefore not a 'fear' needing to be exorcised? Or should we infer that such a fear was so great that they couldn't face its depiction on the stage, that they repressed it? How does one decide?

The *Two Menaechmuses* is a play about two long-lost twins with (confusingly) the same name. It served as a model for Shakespeare's *A Comedy of Errors*. The Menaechmus who lives in Epidamnus seems over-concerned with gaining the love of those around him with cash. The Menaechmus from Syracuse is visiting Epidamnus. He finds himself accidentally enjoying the fruits of Epidamnian Menaechmus' spending. General hilarity ensues. McCarthy argues that Epidamnian Menaechmus shows how *not* to run a household because of his folly in negotiating with his subordinates, including a courtesan (2000: 35ff.). Syracusan Menaechmus, on the other hand, is shown to be in clear control of his slave Messenio: he is a winner, not a loser. Is McCarthy correct? Even if Epidamnian Menaechmus is foolish in 'negotiating' with his subordinates (interestingly Plautus doesn't show him 'negotiating' with his own slaves), it is questionable whether Syracusan Menaechmus' relationship with his slave Messenio actually shows the 'right' way to do things. Messenio does show a (sometimes cloying) loyalty (e.g. *The Two Menaechmuses* 966ff.). Even McCarthy, however, has to admit he occasionally talks back to his master (e.g. *The Two Menaechmuses* 247ff.: why portray this if the aim was to show his proper subservience?). She is also forced to underplay the degree to which Messenio *asks* for his freedom (*The Two*

Menaechmuses 1023ff.). He therefore does precisely what McCarthy claims he shouldn't be doing – negotiating with his master (albeit, farcically, with the wrong twin!). As McCarthy herself implied, rather than see the two brothers as representing the 'right' and 'wrong' way of going about things, one can see *both* as 'incomplete' characters (the Syracusan brother in particular comes close to behaving like a 'clever slave' rather than gentleman). Neither is a model for proper behaviour.

Even if McCarthy were correct in her reading of the relationship between Messenio and his master, however, she still faces an awkward problem. McCarthy argued that slavery was by definition essentially an economic relationship, not one based on loyalty (2000: 37). Loyalty cannot be bought, she believed: treating slaves as commodities ignored their humanity, the only basis on which loyalty could exist. Here is Plautus, however, apparently pretending that slavery *was* something which could be based on loyalty. As with Thalmann's reading of the *The Captives*, so McCarthy's reading of the *The Two Menaechmuses* suggested that Romans would have seen a reassuring message in Plautus' work. McCarthy argued, however, that this is can be done only by 'sleight of hand'. Only by *pretending* that slavery could be based on loyalty could the problems raised in the play be solved. One could, once again, introduce ideas of the 'repression of fears', but the fact remains that her reading of the play requires the Romans being duped by this 'sleight of hand'. There is an alternative possibility: that Romans actually *did* feel a degree of loyalty existed between themselves and their domestic slaves. Slaves might indeed be property but were something more as well.

The possibility of 'negotiation' between master and slave clearly existed. James Scott has shown the multiple, sometimes well-hidden, ways in which oppressed groups can negotiate with those who exploit them, even if no one would suggest that this gives them equality (Scott 1985, 1990). But does Plautus really show a fear of the possibility of such 'negotiation'? How far did the Romans really have an 'anxiety' about the 'negotiation' of control? Was 'negotiation' (and the system of rewards it entailed) part of the pathology of slavery (a deviation from the norm) or was it simply a natural part of its functioning? If Romans never imagined that they had 'absolute control' over their slaves, they would not have felt its absence. McCarthy's 'contradiction' in the slave/ master relationship may rest more on modern views about the nature of the 'essence' (or reality) of slavery, than on what the Romans thought. One could argue that negotiation was seen as the *essence* of the system, especially given the possible levels of manumission and the significance of incentives such as the *peculium*. Comedy *can* indicate deep-rooted fears within a society, but does it indicate this *particular* fear?

If I am raising difficulties with all current interpretations of the slave in Roman comedy, it is not to suggest that all views are equally plausible (for an *im*plausible interpretation, see e.g. Dunkin 1946), or that one can learn nothing from comedy. It offers important information on topics such as the domestic duties of slaves. There is also a clear connection between slavery and indecency, and the free who behave immorally are often described using slave terms. That need not, however, imply a great deal of immoral behaviour from real slaves. It could operate more as an ideological mechanism to differentiate free and slave (with the slave as the opposite of the 'moral' citizen). Of course the stereotype *could* have arisen either from lived experience or from ideological needs or from a mixture of both. The evidence of Roman comedy itself, once again, can support more than one hypothesis. But does Plautus really help Romans negotiate their fear of their slaves? Clearly many modern authors want to believe this, and the evidence allows them to do so. But *should* they believe it? Or should we, while accepting it as a possibility, also accept the weaknesses of that evidence?

Let us return to Keith Bradley. We saw his criticisms of some recent interpretations of the slave in Roman literature. In 2000, however, he published his own analysis of the image of slavery in Apuleius' *Golden Ass*, a novel of the second century AD. Lucius, an over-curious traveller, finds himself magically transformed into an ass. He is captured by bandits and then sold from household to household, being thoroughly abused and beaten along the way. Finally the goddess Isis helps him regain his human shape and his freedom. Bradley argued that Lucius' transformation into an ass reflected the 'animalisation' of the slave. 'Animalisation', he argued, was both a useful tool for slaveowners and also reflected the dehumanising experience of the newly enslaved. The text also illustrated both the viciousness of slavery and the indomitable will of the slave to fight back (the ass has his revenge on some of his tormentors and will eventually regain his humanity).

Bradley, reflecting his criticism of Fitzgerald, attempted to provide wide contextual evidence for the 'animalisation' of slaves by the Romans. He noted, for example, the bracketing together of slaves and animals by agricultural writers and by lawyers (Bradley 2000: 110-11). None of this, however, shows that the 'animalisation' of the slave is part of Apuleius' strategy in this text, or even that it was a general social view. The apparent willingness to free large numbers of slaves and grant them citizenship could be used to argue against it. Lawyers might bracket slaves with animals, but we saw that Roman law of its nature was likelier than the rest of society to view slaves from the viewpoint of property. It also afforded slaves protection that wasn't afforded to animals (e.g. Suetonius, *Claudius* 25.2; *Digest* 1.12.1.1, 1.12.1.8, 48.8.11.1; Justinian, *Institutes* 1.8.2). The connection between slaves and animals in Roman agricultural writers may be primarily technical (slaves and animals represented the most important types of movable property one could find on a farm). One of the agricultural writers, Columella, specifically differentiates slaves and animals: he doesn't, so far as I am aware, chat with or encourage the latter (see e.g. Columella, *On Agriculture* 1.8.15-18).

Lucius' story could, indeed, be read (like the story of Vedius Pollio's slave) as a *critique* of those who 'animalise' the slave. It might show that animalisation was a *possible* strategy, but not that it was necessarily prevalent or socially acceptable. We are, after all, on the side of Lucius, the 'person' being beaten. Similarly when Apuleius (*Golden Ass* 8.22) records the tale of a slave-adulterer being left to be eaten by ants (which Bradley sees as both grisly and 'normative', 2000: 122), the point may be its very shockingness (as with the stories of gruesome violence towards *free* people: *Golden Ass* 1.13-19).

5. 'I too *want* to tell a story ...'

Bradley's argument that Lucius' resistance and final redemption indicates a recognition by Roman slaveowners that their slaves could fight back (2000: 120-1), raises the same difficulty we saw in McCarthy's discussion of the figure of the slave-lover. Did the audience engage with Lucius as a figure representing slaves in general, or as 'one of us' who has had the misfortune to be (wrongly) enslaved but who retained some of the skills and abilities that make 'us' who 'we' are?

Apuleius' text can certainly be used to help us imagine what it was like to be a Roman slave. So could a modern novel or a movie. It serves as a useful metaphor for what *was* (if one can deploy the requisite supporting evidence: see the doubts expressed above) or *might have been* (if one cannot). A classicist might be happy with the mind-expanding possibilities of the latter, an historian probably not. Ironically, the difficulties Bradley faced in his analysis of Lucius' story echo some of his own critique of Fitzgerald discussed earlier in this chapter. The work on Apuleius also illustrates, once again, the way a stress on slave resistance apparently 'writes itself into' many modern analyses. Bradley's desire to rescue the experience of the slave (as we saw in the last chapter) is a noble one. We might find repugnant the idea that the 'real' slave has disappeared into the imagination of the slaveowner. We may, however, have to accept the fact that it sometimes *has* disappeared and be clearer about where that may leave our own historical reconstructions.

Literary readings can, therefore, offer interesting new interpretative possibilities. Far from solving the methodological problems raised in the last chapter, however, they both reflect and intensify them. Keith Hopkins certainly recognised the difficulties involved. Having given his analysis of the *Life of Aesop*, he continued (1993: 22):

> To be sure, this is only one interpretation of a story. I cannot be sure that it is right. But interpretative history flourishes on precisely those ambiguities which the substantivist (conservative) historian of objective truth finds least comfortable, or more objectionable.

'Interpretative history' therefore seems to have different rules from 'objective truth'. In an accompanying footnote he refers to the 'intellectual battle' between 'conservative positivists' and 'interpretative pluralists'. One suspects that anyone attempting to write a narrative of ancient slavery was included under 'conservative positivists'. 'Interpretative pluralists' most probably included all those trained to look for multiple meanings in texts. Hopkins actually gives his reader little reason to support one side rather than the other in this 'battle' (though his use of the term 'conservative' perhaps gives us a clue as to who we are supposed to support).

Hopkins may have felt that he did not need to be more explicit. While doubting the value of 'anecdotal history', he still tacitly believed there was a background context into which his ideas about Aesop would fit. Like Bradley, he felt there was 'hard' evidence which provided boundaries for 'interpretative pluralists'. However, unlike Bradley, he did not feel this 'hard' evidence was made up of particular types of trustworthy sources or archaeological material. It was constituted instead by statistical probability. I would like to finish my examination of the range of different approaches to

Roman slavery by examining statistical, demographic, approaches. Can they give us a more 'scientific' basis on which to rest our hypotheses about Roman slaves?

6

A Scientific Approach to Ancient Slavery?

The last twenty years have seen the increasing prominence of a very different style of history writing from that examined in our last few chapters. It is an approach which seems to promise an escape from literary evidence which can be used (apparently) to ornament both sides of an argument. It focuses instead on statistics and on probability.

While our knowledge of the date of our own death is (usually and thankfully) vague, the *probable* mortality and fertility patterns of large groups of people are easier to predict. Those who investigate the demography of the ancient world do not claim to deal in exact answers, only such probabilities. It is these, they argue, that allow one to talk sensibly about the plausible and the probable rather than running around in circles trying to interpret a character in a Roman comedy. Their tables of statistics certainly *look* scientific. Let us examine their approach by focussing on just one important question they may help to answer: where did the Romans get their slaves, particularly at the height of empire after AD 14?

The three main ways of entering slavery were probably capture in war or by pirates, being born a slave, and being left to die by one's parents but being found and then raised as a slave. Adding up the number of references Romans made to each possibility would probably tell us more about what interested contemporary writers than proving which was the most important. Keith Bradley (1987) argued that all three potential sources were important, but that the evidence might be so impressionistic we can never hope to reach any more exact answer (cf. Parkin 1992: 121-2 and Frier 2000: 808). Walter Scheidel argued that as many as 75-80% of Rome's slaves were the children of slaves (Scheidel 1997: 167). William Harris believed that this figure was too high and that a significant proportion of Rome's slaves came instead from outside the empire or from children left to die inside the empire (see Harris 1980 and especially 1999: 62-3). I want to look at the debate in the late 1990s between Harris and Scheidel, but I need to begin by introducing some of the tools demographers use to examine populations.

Demographers use something called 'Model Life Tables' to predict the age profile of a given population (see Coale, Demeny and Vaughan 1983). These Tables are based on different geographical areas which are able to supply us with reliable statistical information. 'Model South' is popular with ancient historians since it is based on Mediterranean statistics and assumes high infant mortality, apparently the case in ancient Rome. 'Model West' is even more popular. It is an average of a whole series of 'Life Tables' and is probably the safest to generalise from in the absence of solid information. Each 'Model' is then subdivided into different population tables determined by the average life expectancy at birth. Life expectancy in modern Britain is now over 70. So far as we can tell it was much lower in pre-industrial societies (largely because of the effect of high infant mortality decreasing the overall average). Most of our (inadequate) ancient evidence tends to produce a range of possibilities of between 20 and 30 years, with the most probable average at the lower end. This corresponds to 'Model West' [or 'South'] Level 2.

For a society simply to reproduce itself each woman must, on average, give birth to a female child who survives long enough to be a mother in her turn. The problem for an ancient Roman family would have been the high chance of a daughter dying young. To provide a replacement, the average woman in Italy would have had to give birth to an average of three girls (if Model West Level 2 is anything like a good match for the ancient Roman empire). That means about *six* births (both male and female) in total. That might seem a high number (certainly if you are a woman) but without it the population would have collapsed.

It is time to make a few more assumptions. Walter Scheidel estimated that the population of the Roman empire ultimately reached about 60 million (1997: 158). He assumed that about 6 million (or 10%) of the population were slaves (we will examine some of his evidence later). He argued that the population outside the empire from which the Romans could import slaves was perhaps 20 million, or one third of that of the empire (1997: 159-60). This figure is obviously open to challenge. The Romans, however, generally expanded in most directions until they hit ecological boundaries that made further advance uneconomic (e.g. deserts), or else met political entities which could successfully resist them (e.g. Parthia). It seems logical, therefore, to suppose that the area from which the Romans could draw an external supply of slaves was considerably less populous than the empire itself. Crucially it is not precise numbers that are important here, but the assumptions Scheidel makes about the *ratios* between free and slave within the empire (9:1) and between the (exploitable) population inside and outside the empire (3:1).

Could the slave population have been maintained without needing to draw substantially on the free population for replacements? To answer the question we need to know how many babies slave women had each year, and the proportion of the 6 million slaves who either died or were freed each year and who would therefore need replacing. Literary evidence doesn't give us this information. This is, however, where demography proves its worth.

First, how many slaves died each year? Scheidel assumed that slaves didn't live as long as free people (though cf. Scheidel 2005: 74, 76). Comparative statistics from modern slave societies in the Caribbean and the US suggest 2-5% more deaths among slaves than free people every year. Scheidel chose a lower estimate for Rome, 1% extra (1997: 163-4, with n31).

It is difficult to guess how many slaves were freed. Scheidel decided to use a thought experiment. He imagined three different possible levels of manumission, one 'low', one 'intermediate', one 'high'. Let's look at his 'intermediate' model. This assumed that 10% of all slaves are freed at age 25 and 10% of the remainder every five years thereafter on average (1997: 160). Freeing slaves would have increased the numbers of replacement slaves needed each year and also have decreased the number of slave children born (1997: 163). One might ask why. The key is the legal status of children. The child of a slave was a slave. But if a woman was freed at the age of 30 (for example) her future children were generally free and so lost to the slave population. The exact proportion lost depended on how often and how early female slaves were manumitted. Hence Scheidel's different models.

If Romans did have anything like Scheidel's 'intermediate' level of manumission, they would have required the equivalent of just under 320,000 babies a year to make into slaves (1997: 164). If one assumes that the proportion of female to male slaves was roughly equal, Scheidel expected just over 200,000 slave births a year. This would still have left a deficit of 110,000-120,000 future slaves. They had to be found among the free population either inside or outside the empire.

Scheidel assumed that no more than half of these replacements came from the free population outside the empire (1997: 164). He argued that any higher number would have put ludicrous pressure on the population there because (as we saw) it was possibly only a third of the size of that within the empire. 40,000 captives a year would have filled half of the 110,000-120,000 deficit. That may not seem like half, but it is. Infancy was the most dangerous period in life, but imported slaves would have been older. Since captives had generally already survived infant mortality, fewer were required than babies.

That still left almost 60,000 'baby equivalents' needed from *within* the empire. Adult self-enslavement was known, but it is difficult to judge how frequently it happened. The exposure of children (who might then be raised as slaves) was probably more common. Scheidel argued that is hardly reasonable to assume that *all* Roman families left children out to die because they couldn't afford to raise them: the richest quarter of the population would surely not have faced this problem. The potential 'reservoir' for exposed free children was therefore not the 54 million of the free population but only the poorest threequarters of it, perhaps 40 million (1997: 159). Those 40 million probably produced (according to Model West Level 2) about 1.8 million children each year (1997: 160). In order to fill the gap in slave supply approximately 60,000, or about 1 in 30, must have become slaves (1997: 164). We noted earlier that, simply to keep the population stable, Roman mothers must have had an average of 6 births each. *On average* therefore 1 in 5 mothers would (at some point of their life) have had to abandon one of their children to slavery if Scheidel's 'intermediate model' approximates to reality. Of course, not all the children exposed would have survived, increasing the number of abandoned children required. Scheidel suggested that perhaps half died, so 1 in 15 surviving children must become slaves. This implies that, on average, 1 in 2 or 1 in 3 of all mothers in the Roman empire would have had to expose a child to produce the required number of slaves, something he saw as straining credulity.

Scheidel's essential argument was that this would have been a phenomenon of unheralded enormity and pain. We ought, therefore, to see copious reference to that pain in our sources. We don't. This suggested to Scheidel that it is unlikely infant exposure was such an important source of slaves. Scheidel therefore argued, by a process of elimination, that breeding *must* have been the primary source of slaves, and so even his 'Intermediate' model, assuming 67% replacement by breeding, was too conservative. The real figure may have been even higher.

There are a number of implications. If 75-80% of slave replacements came from breeding, female slaves could not have been freed as often as the 'intermediate' model suggests. Hence Scheidel developed what he saw as a rather more realistic 'low' model assuming 10% manumission at age 30 (not 25) and 10% manumission for surviving slaves every 5 years thereafter (1997: 166). He also allowed for a smaller extra slave mortality figure than his 'intermediate' model (0.5% rather than 1.0%). Taken together, these changes in his model would allow for 82% of slaves to be bred from existing slaves, with the remaining 55,000 coming from the free population within and without the empire. The key point is that the Romans would have had good reason to prevent female slaves of childbearing age from gaining freedom. Scheidel felt that there was evidence from some Egyptian census statistics to back this up, though he recognised that the numbers involved (44 females) were rather small for a detailed statistical examination (161-2; cf. Bradley 1978).

If Scheidel is correct, freedwomen (and, by extension, freedmen, who seem to have preferred to marry within their own status group) would have had little chance to contribute to the genetic makeup of the population (see 1997: 167-8). This contradicts the arguments we saw in Chapter 1 that the population of Rome became a bastardised slavish rabble. If correct, Scheidel's model allows us to move beyond the biases of our sources (and, to some extent, the biases of modern historians) towards a more objective picture of ancient slavery.

6. A Scientific Approach to Ancient Slavery?

There are, however, some potential criticisms of Scheidel's approach. William Harris (1999) criticised it for: (1) not giving enough emphasis to evidence for slave-imports in our literary sources; (2) exaggerating the number of children born of slaves; (3) underestimating how many free children might have been exposed.

(1) Had Scheidel underplayed the evidence of imports? Probably not. Scheidel accepted that there were perhaps 10,000-15,000 slaves imported each year (1997: 167). This a small fraction of the replacements needed, but still very noticeable to contemporaries and it would explain the number of comments about imports we find in our sources. On the other hand, Scheidel's arguments *against* high levels of importation could themselves be attacked. Here is how Scheidel put his case against imports being a high as 40,000 per annum (1997: 164n34):

> The occidental slave trade to the Americas reached an annual average of 70,000 in the late eighteenth century ... More than ten million Africans reached the New World as slaves from 1500 to 1900. The rate of intake for the Roman empire assumed here would have been considerably larger in the long run (at four million per century) – once again, a rather unlikely supposition.

Should this comparison rule out higher Roman slave imports?

(2) Was Scheidel assuming unreasonably high levels of fertility among slaves? Harris argued that for Scheidel to be correct, slave girls would have had to breed at quite striking

131

rates. He gave several sets of figures for the average number of births required because, like Scheidel, there was an important variable he couldn't pin down: the ratio of female to male slaves (Harris 1999: 67ff.). The higher the proportion of male slaves, the fewer the number of potential slave mothers, and the higher the number of children required of each mother. The evidence seems to suggest more male slaves than female slaves (though, *pace* Harris, this might reflect a lack of interest in mentioning women rather than reality). Harris argued that, for Scheidel's model to work, slave women would have had to produce as many as seven or eight children each. That was, perhaps, several higher than the average for free women. Harris argued that this was unlikely. Conditions for slaves may not have favoured access to partners or privacy nor have encouraged the creation of large families (1999: 65ff.). Scheidel recognised these potential problems, but argued that the USA in the nineteenth century showed that the natural reproduction of a slave population was *possible* (Scheidel 1997: 168-9; cf. 2005: 71-3 and 75). The important question, Scheidel knew, was whether Rome, at least in this respect, was similar to the USA. He believed it was. Harris believed it wasn't. Harris argued that Scheidel had not taken into account the harshness of Roman slavery. In an echo of some of the debates we have seen in earlier chapters Harris stressed the inhumanity of Roman slavery (1999: esp. 68). Scheidel, on the other hand, argued as follows (1997: 169):

In the absence of statistical data, structure and fertility of Roman slave families remain obscure. The evidence from the Roman census returns suggests that slave fertility was

132

similar to that of all free women, though well below that of all married women: Bagnall and Frier op. cit. (n. 16), 158. However, this information comes from households with only a few slaves where family formation may have been difficult; moreover, we must allow for the possibility that some children of slave mothers did not appear in the returns because they had already been sold (ibid., 158n. 85). As for larger slaveholdings in Roman Italy, there is only sparse impressionist evidence: App., *BC* 1.1.7 takes it for granted that slaves on large agricultural estates would have numerous offspring, a notion that is consistent with Varro, *RR* 2.10.6 and Colum., *RR* 1.8.19. The same may have been true for large urban households.

Both sides quote ancient evidence to show that breeding either was or wasn't widespread. We are dragged back into the kind of discussion we were hoping to escape by using demography. Harris's difficulty, however, is that Scheidel's US example does at least show that breeding was a *possible* way of reproducing a slave population.

(3) Was Scheidel underestimating the number of exposed freeborn children? He was aware that nineteenth-century Europe had seen some extremely high rates of exposure. He believed, however, that these were unusual, the product of the foundation of foundling hospitals in urban areas. This might have increased the likelihood of exposure, since parents might be more willing to abandon a child if they believed it would survive (165n37). The Romans didn't have such hospitals:

'... there is nothing to suggest that the modern data could be of much relevance for antiquity.'

We are here, of course, sucked back into trying to decide which set of potential comparative modern statistics is the 'exception' – Milan's 30% exposure rate in the nineteenth century, or Lombardy's 4.8%. While Romans didn't have foundling hospitals, they might, nonetheless, have used places to expose children that they expected to be visited. Here the difficulty is Scheidel's. Harris has shown that high levels of child exposure *could* have formed an important source of slaves.

Harris may have successfully raised a number of doubts about some of Scheidel's arguments. This did not mean, however, that he was necessarily successful in proving that slave breeding was less important than Scheidel imagined. The problem was that Harris shared some of his opponent's starting premises. His estimate of the proportion of slaves in the population of the empire, 15%+, was even *higher* than Scheidel's (see Harris 1999: 65). The higher the proportion of slaves, the higher the number of replacements required each year, and the less plausible the filling of the gap with exposed freeborn children and with imports (as noted by Scheidel 1997: 165). How could the periphery of the empire supply such numbers? Why doesn't child exposure figure even more prominently in our sources if it was at very high levels? Scheidel was winning on points. But perhaps we should look at the rules of the game. Scheidel's position actually rested on a number of key assumptions which were left unchallenged by Harris. He was perhaps right to leave them unchallenged. Changing one or all of them, however, would have important effects on all the impressive statistics quoted. First I will suggest ways in which one *could* change the rules of the game, but probably *shouldn't* (I will give reasons why not). Then I will suggest one very major 'rule of the game' that really might be challenged. First, the more 'minor' rules.

(1) Both authors believed Roman life expectancy was in the low 20s. If it was actually closer to 30 there would be a significantly higher potential reservoir of babies among the free and at the same time fewer slave replacements would be needed. That, however, would seem to run counter to most of the indicators we do have on mortality.

(2) If slaves lived as long as free people (or even longer), the number of necessary replacements would also fall. Longer life expectancy for slaves is possible (they were, after all, an investment to be looked after), but it does, nonetheless, seem unlikely.

(3) Could slave women have produced significantly more children than free women? Again, this is possible, but, given what we know of slave living conditions, perhaps not plausible.

(4) Scheidel didn't argue that *all* the free population might have exposed babies, only the poorest threequarters. For his intermediate model to work, 1 in 30 children *from poor families* would have to be exposed to be raised as possible slaves. This is literally '1 in 40' of *all* children. However, while this makes some difference to the statistics, it is not a massive difference. One might also note also that some women might have *regularly* exposed their children (reducing the *average* number who would have done so).

(5) Scheidel assumed that more than half all exposed children died. If a significantly higher proportion than 40-50% of exposed children survived to be raised as slaves, however, one would require a much lower number of exposures to satisfy the need for new slaves. That said, such a high survival rate does seem unlikely.

(6) Could more slaves have come from outside the empire than Scheidel believed? 70,000 imported slaves a year would produce perhaps a third of all requirements. One might then argue for another third from breeding and a third from exposure. It would, however, as Scheidel noted, have come at a dramatic demographic cost to the populations outside the empire. We also have little way of proving it.

We have already seen that there is, however, another, vital, assumption in Scheidel's arguments. He assumed that 10% of the population of the empire were slaves. Imagine, however, that only 5% were slaves. One would then require only half the number of replacements Scheidel suggested (now approximately 150,000 each year). It would also, however, make exposure and importation more plausible, and breeding less vital, as major sources of slaves (see Harris 1999: 64). 40,000 imports might then produce about a third of the replacements. Exposure rates less than half of Scheidel's intermediate rate could produce a sixth, with half coming from breeding, bringing the situation closer perhaps to that implied by Harris.

The estimate that 10% (or more) of the population were slaves is therefore very important. On what is it based? Very little. There are only two regions of the empire where historians have been prepared to make serious guesses. The first is Italy. In his book *Italian Manpower* Peter Brunt argued (1971: 124):

> In my view we could put the number of slaves at about 3,000,000, out of a total population of no more than 7,500,000 (Cisalpina included). This ratio of slaves to free men is extraordinarily high.

It is indeed high: 40% of the Italian population would have been slaves. That is higher than either Scheidel or Harris initially suggested. It is, however, only an estimate for *Italy*. Italy was the wealthiest part of the empire and probably the likeliest to use slaves. If Brunt were correct we would, however, already be half-way to the 6 million slaves suggested by Scheidel *for the whole empire*. Brunt, however, was principally concerned to undermine an earlier attempt (by Beloch) to argue that 2 million was the *maximum* number of slaves Italy could support. The little evidence he gives for his preferred estimate is surprisingly impressionistic. For example (122):

> Beloch remarked that Spartacus' army never exceeded 120,000. In fact the number of slaves who took part in his rising appears to have been rather larger, say 150,000 ... The loss of so many slaves must have been a grave blow to their employers, but there is no suggestion in our evidence that the *latifundia* were denuded of labour, and I incline to think that we should have heard of this, if it had been the case. This leads me to suppose that the

137

rebels constituted only a small part of the total servile labour force.

There is also reference to a literary source claiming that perhaps a quarter of the population of Pergamum (in Turkey) were slaves, but this throws us back again to the question of the reliability of literary impressions. How would ancient authors have known these figures? And how widely can we generalise from what they say to the whole of the empire?

We need to avoid misunderstandings. There were *a lot* of slaves in Italy (and particularly in Rome). I am not arguing against the idea that they produced the bulk of the wealth of the elite. I am merely pointing out how soft some of the 'statistics' may be, even for Italy. It is worth noting that Wim Jongman (using his own variety of cliometrics) has recently argued that Italian slavery was primarily an urban phenomenon and that the number of rural slaves has been exaggerated (Jongman 2003). Indeed Scheidel himself, following Jongman, now doubts the Brunt figure for Italy, and has argued for a figure perhaps half as large or less (Scheidel 2005, though he may be preparing to lower his estimate of the size of the free population too).

The second area where historians have been prepared to make estimates for the slave population has been Roman Egypt. Surviving census statistics indicate that about 11% of the population was slave. Or do they? One might leave aside traditional arguments that Egypt was not necessarily representative of the rest of the empire (a view difficult to prove or disprove). One might also ignore the sparse number of surviving census returns (1,100 people, including just over

100 slaves, scattered over several centuries). This probably represents less than 0.01% of the total, but modern polling organisations would not necessarily be unhappy with this size of sample. But how representative is the census material? Most of it comes from just two of the 'nomes' or administrative districts of Egypt. Urban areas seem to be over-represented and seem to have had more slaves than rural areas (13% as opposed to 7%). The ratio of male to female (roughly one to two) also seems very odd. It has been argued recently that this is due to the sample being skewed by a small number of households that had a strong bias (for some reason) towards female slaves (Bagnall and Frier 1994: 94). This irregularity is thought-provoking in itself.

To summarise: *if* the slaves made up 10% of the population of the empire, it is highly probable that breeding was the source of the clear majority of slaves and that female slaves were unlikely to be freed while they could produce children. The burden of proof would certainly rest on those who would claim that breeding was *not* the source of most slaves. But the 'if' in the first sentence of this paragraph is critical. If only 5% of the empire's inhabitants were slaves, the proportion of home-bred slaves *may* have been much lower than Scheidel suggested.

I have tried to show that the course of the demographic debate remains very sensitive to its starting premises. Those starting premises are in turn easily affected by the kind of messy debates about the interpretation of sources we saw in earlier chapters. The argument between Scheidel and Harris is massively affected by the estimate of the proportion of slaves within the overall population. Ironically, Scheidel himself may be in the process of re-evaluating this number. Whatever its advantages and disadvantages, however, the demographic approach at least operates by debating the limits of uncertainty, and as such it acts as a good metaphor for how the history of slavery *ought* to be written, even if it isn't. And it does tell us something important. Even if we reduced the proportion of slaves to 5% of the population, breeding would *probably* remain the single most important source for slaves. That means the chance of female slaves gaining their freedom during their child-bearing age was *probably* greatly restricted. We don't therefore live in a 'postmodern' trap of utter uncertainty. On the other hand, we need always to be aware of just how provisional our answers are, and just how much they are determined by conscious and unconscious starting assumptions.

The Greeks Do It (a Bit) Better: The Opportunities of Silence

The approaches examined in previous chapters are not specific to the study of slavery in the Roman empire between 200 BC and AD 200. They can be also be found in research on slavery in the Greek world (particularly Athens) between 500 and 300 BC. One can find similarities, for example, between the work of Siegfried Lauffer and Fridolf Kudlien (Chapter 2), Virginia Hunter and Keith Bradley (Chapter 4), or Madeleine Mactoux and Marguerite Garrido-Hory (Chapter 2). There has been no true equivalent to Elena Shtaerman's particular brand of Marxism (Chapter 3), but one might compare the work of Geoffrey de Ste. Croix. The 'literary' approaches seen in Chapter 5 are mirrored in work by scholars such as Denise Eileen McCoskey and particularly Page duBois, some of whose work is discussed in detail below. Greek historians have, however, been largely unwilling to indulge in the kind of demographic debates about slavery we saw in Chapter 6 (though see Gallant 1991). Recently, however, specialists on Greek slavery have started to add something extra of their own to the mix. American-based authors such as duBois, Stephen Johnstone and Peter Hunt have begun to discuss the implications of what might be *missing* from our evidence.

Their approaches open up exciting new opportunities. They also, however, illustrate the strength of 'traditional' narratives of ancient slavery that still sometimes manage to seep into their work despite their sophistication.

Steven Johnstone and the importance of silence

In 1998 Steven Johnstone examined the difficulties and possibilities of writing the history of slaves (and women) from speeches surviving from Athenian law courts of the fifth and fourth centuries BC. Typically the arguments from only one of the two sides involved in a dispute survive, so the facts of the case can be difficult to establish. More importantly, only Athenian male citizens normally had access to the courts. Any conflict that reached the courts was therefore regarded as a dispute between such men rather than between men and women or masters and slaves (Johnstone 1998: 222, 225). Women and slaves were generally invisible, but this may reflect the ideology of the citizen males more than the reality outside the courts (234, cf. 222):

> The silence of the sources was not merely an unfortunate effect of free men's power; it was also one of its foundations.

Lysias' *On a wound by premeditation* describes a conflict between two men over a slave girl (Johnstone 1998: 221-2). There is only a hint that the girl had any active role (Lysias 4.8 and 4.17, where it is claimed that she favoured the plaintiff). Johnstone, however, wondered how much of the girl's story we might be missing – could she in fact have initiated the conflict between her admirers (1998: 222)?

Demosthenes' *Against Olympiodorus* is the story of a row between Callistratus and his brother-in-law (Johnstone 1998: 230-1). Callistratus claims that Olympiodorus had reneged on a deal to split an inheritance. He hints that Olympidorus has been influenced by his mistress whom he has bought out of slavery and kept in luxury (Demosthenes 48.55). Johnstone argued that perhaps (1998: 232):

... since power can both constrain and enable ... what we see in the case of Olympiodorus' love is the ability of one oppressed person to strategically deploy its enabling capacity.

Finally, Demosthenes' *Against Neaera* describes how Neaera allegedly rose from foreign slave-prostitute to become (illegally) the wife of an important Athenian politician, Stephanus (Johnstone 1998: 232-3). Stephanus had intervened to protect Neara against a former client, Phrynion (Johnstone 1998: 232):

The inability of a legal narrative to represent Neaera as a subject stands as an obstacle to recovering her experiences as a slave and as a woman; more than this, though, it partially constituted those experiences. Neaera does not seem to have been an impotent pawn of the men around her. Indeed, she enrolled Stephanus as her protector precisely to more effectively stand up to Phrynion.

Johnstone argued that we need not simply accept the traditional view of slaves as passive objects, especially when there are hints of a very different reality. This is a vital and important point. What we do, having established this is, however, much less clear. It might be true that (229):

In many of these cases, there is enough information to suspect that slaves may have been disputants with interests of their own.

But the key word here is 'suspect'. The stories given in the speeches may indeed illustrate examples of 'hidden' slave action, but they can also be explained in other ways. The hint that the girl in Lysias 4 was biased towards the prosecution might indeed imply that she had an active role in the case. It might, however, also help undermine any (indirect) testimony from her side. It might also suggest that the prosecutor is being manipulated by a woman, something that would put him in a poor light. As Johnstone noted, Athenian law could equate 'being under the influence of a woman' with insanity (229). Callistratus may be insinuating something similar of Olympiodorus in Demosthenes 48, and Apollodorus of Neaera's husband in Demosthenes 59. In that last case one should also note that Neaera may not even have been a slave prostitute. The prosecutor, Apollodorus (himself the son of a freedman), was an enemy of Neaera's husband, Stephanus. Athenian citizens could choose legitimate wives only from among Athenian freeborn women. If Neaera could be portrayed successfully as a non-citizen, Stephanus' family would have been utterly ruined. So, these stories may indicate that slave-women were more active than our sources generally claim, but it is also possible that the speaker in each case had a good motive for making things look that way. Do they therefore illustrate the tip of the iceberg, suggesting that slave 'agency' could be a real problem for masters, or that such agency was a shocking exception which undermined the reputation of any citizen male who let it happen? Or something in between? Yes, we must be ready to read 'against the grain' of our sources. Moving, however, from the recognition of a silence (and an understanding of the possible ideological importance of such a silence) to any judgement of the realities behind it remains hideously difficult.

Peter Hunt and modern and ancient 'silencing'

In his *Slaves, Warfare, and Ideology in the Greek Historians*, Peter Hunt, like Johnstone, argued that the silences and emphases of the ancient sources should not dictate our view of the past. Most modern historians before Hunt had argued that classical Greeks were extremely reluctant to recruit slaves into their armies and navies. He showed that even though ancient writers say little *explicitly* on the subject, there are enough passing comments to suggest that the military use of slaves was actually widespread. For example, the historian Thucydides mentioned slaves deserting the Athenian fleet at Syracuse in 413 (Thucydides 7.13), even though he wrote nothing about their prior recruitment (Hunt 1998: 99-100). Hunt tried to explain why Greek historians chose to give as little stress as possible to the use of slaves in war and also to slave rebellion (particularly where the free had encouraged it). He suggested a number of important ideological reasons. He argued that Greek historians wished to reinforce the supposed differences between slave and free, for example portraying slaves as passive and as cowards, utterly different from brave citizens (3):

> Paradoxically, such representations may also assuage the insecurity of masters living in dangerous proximity to their slaves.

This mirrored, he suggested, the US development of the 'Sambo' stereotype of the cowardly and obsequious slave (160-4, here 160-1):

> On the one hand, the practice of slavery encouraged certain patterns of behavior on the part of the slave. On the other hand, masters had a need to despise the people they oppressed. The more that slaves seemed not to be content with, or not to deserve their condition, the more intensely masters clung to the stereotype of a childish, cowardly Sambo.

There was also the 'Nat' (sc. Turner), the rebellious slave of US slave mythology (162). The more fear slaveowners had of 'Nat', the greater their need to believe in the cowardly 'Sambo' (163):

> At stake in the maintenance of the slave stereotype was any confidence that threat of punishment could deter your own slave from killing you.

Hunt therefore suggested that Greek historical writers underplayed the active role played by slaves. I will focus on his discussion of Thucydides, his most important and convincing example. Thucydides, we are told, downplayed the significance of slaves on a series of occasions during his description of the Peloponnesian War between Athens and Sparta which lasted from 431 to 404 BC. He did so, argued Hunt, not because he was a propagandist, but because these episodes cut against his world-view (121ff.). Greek civic unity was underpinned by the maintenance of the distinction between slave and free (132ff.). The Peloponnesian War saw that civic unity undermined by civil wars and by the importation of slaves into the supposedly citizen world of the military. Thucydides' response was to 'push' slaves to the 'margin' of his narrative (135) and (133):

> ... the ideological insistence on the dichotomy of slave and citizen suggests anxiety both about the boundary between slave and free and about the unity of citizens. Both problems are likely to have been particularly intense during and directly after the Peloponnesian War, the period in which Thucydides wrote.

Let us examine a few of Hunt's examples.

During the first stage of the Peloponnesian War an Athenian fleet set up a fort on an island (Sphacteria) just off the coast of Messenia, then controlled by Athens' enemy Sparta. Thucydides writes as if the fortification was the product of chance, of an accidental landing caused by a storm (Thucydides 4.2ff.). The effects on Sparta were, however, dramatic. Almost 300 soldiers, including 120 of Sparta's precious citizens, were captured while desperately attempting to retake the island (Thucydides 4.38). The landings also stimulated unrest among Sparta's servant population ('helots'), in the surrounding region. Hunt argued that the expedition (and its key effects) must have been planned, not just the product of luck, and that Thucydides' narrative largely conceals how the 'helots' constituted the 'Achilles' heel' of Spartan society (Hunt 1998: 71-5, 79-82).

Are we faced here with an 'ideological' suppression of the truth? Possibly, but, again, there are other potential readings. The 'Sphacteria' episode did not necessarily fit easily with the kind of themes famously developed by Thucydides (e.g. the arrogance of empire, 3.36ff. or 5.84ff.). Thucydides, like other Greeks writing history, was not just producing a narrative 'as it actually was', but trying to teach lessons, lessons for citizens. Slaves were comparatively unimportant in such a narrative. That is a form of censorship, but it need have nothing to do with any 'fear' of the boundary between slave and free being undermined. Thucydides may also have had specific *political* reasons for treating the episode as he did. It ran counter to the strategy of avoiding land engagements supposedly advocated by Thucydides' hero Pericles (see Thucydides 1.141ff. and 2.65). Worse still, its success was to cement the reputation of Thucydides' enemy Cleon. This gave him every reason to suggest that the success was down to pure luck and to emphasise its impact as little as possible. Hunt accepted this (1998: 75):

An awareness of Thucydides' reluctance to dwell upon

the incitement of slave revolts intersects with and reinforces explanations linking Pylos to riskier, un-Periclean war strategies and their proponents.

Although it would be simplistic to argue that Thucydides' reluctance to discuss the incitement of slave revolts is the sole cause of his strange narrative of Pylos, it probably did contribute.

Probably?

Thucydides may actually have been correct in placing his emphasis where he did. The Pylos operation didn't determine the course of the war: Athens eventually lost. While it is possible to argue (particularly with hindsight and from a modern sociological perspective) that helots were Sparta's weak point (Hunt 1998: 71), it is equally possible to argue that demographic or diplomatic issues were much more important in her long-term fate.

Let us look at another element in the 'pattern' of omissions. An Athenian army invaded Sicily and then besieged Syracuse in 414/413. Polyaenus, writing centuries later, wrote that hundreds of Syracusan slaves rebelled (*Stratagems* 1.43.1). We have no reason to believe he invented this episode, but Thucydides, who wrote exhaustively on the siege, ignored it entirely. This could be an example of the suppression of an unwelcome fact, especially if the Athenians had helped incite the slaves (Hunt 1998: 105-6). However, there is, once again, another possible explanation. The rebellion didn't affect the result of the siege. Nor did it fit Thucydides' theme of the journey from arrogance to destruction of the Athenian expedition to Sicily. Thucydides' estimation of the 'unimportance' still tells us something about his world-view and his lack of interest in slaves as anything other than passive objects or simple chattels. It also suggests there may be many examples of rebellion our sources simply chose not to report. It does not, however, necessarily imply that Thucydides left out the story because it was somehow ideologically threatening.

As a final example, Hunt noted that Thucydides mentions the difficulties that Sparta and her allies had in finding rowers for their fleet. He ignores, Hunt claimed, one of the solutions, the recruitment of slaves (1998: 84-7). Thucydides' omission is 'motivated' (56): he recognised the importance of slave rowers, but chose to ignore them as much as possible. This may be true, but one can, again, offer a different interpretation. Slave rowers may have been significant to each navy, but there is again a good case that the determinants of victory and defeat lay elsewhere. Firstly, in the decision of the Persian empire to weaken Athens by supplying money to the Spartans for ships and hiring rowers. Secondly, in the defection of Athenian allies and the subsequent losses to Athens' fleet and manpower. And, finally, in the strategic and political mistakes made by the Athenians themselves. Thucydides may have omitted slave rowers because (possibly correctly) he didn't see them as a key factor.

Hunt claimed that this pattern of 'suppression' can also be seen in the work of other Greek historians such as Herodotus and Xenophon (26-39, 177ff., esp. 180). The passages cited are subject, however, to the same kind of debate we have just seen with Thucydides. And even if one *were* to accept that

7. The Greeks Do It (a Bit) Better

Thucydides' 'anxieties' led him to edit out episodes where slaves seemed unsettlingly prominent, we still need to ask how important this is. It is one of Hunt's great achievements to show just willing both sides in the Peloponnesian War were to use slaves (chs 4-7). Thucydides' alleged touchiness about the blurring of the slave/ free divide was, admittedly, not peculiar to him (note, e.g., the attack on granting citizenship to slaves who had fought for Athens mounted in the play *The Frogs* by the comic playwright Aristophanes). On the other hand, many of those actively engaged in politics seem to have had rather less concern about the use of slaves (and the purity of the slave/ free divide) than he did. How important a stream of opinion does Thucydides therefore 'represent'?

The line between slave and free may therefore have been a little less 'threatened', and the 'anxieties' among owners rather less severe, than Hunt argued. One can only heartily agree with Hunt that modern historians have underestimated the use of slaves in ancient Greek warfare. He has shown that we should not (and need not) simply accept the silences (or emphases) of our sources. His negative points, e.g. his attack on the lazy belief that fighting for one's master implied loyalty, are vital. Hunt discovered something important about the way Greek historians read slavery, but his *explanation* for this shows it is sometimes easier to undermine old assumptions than prove new ones. He made a fundamental contribution to our knowledge but also illustrated the limits of that knowledge and our desire to fill the gaps with a particular type of story.

Page duBois and filling the silence

Page duBois' *Slaves and Other Objects* argued that both ancient and modern authors have conspired, for different reasons, to write slaves out of the story of antiquity. She was clearly aware, therefore, of the difficulty of writing their history (2003: 22):

> I don't think we will ever have access to 'what slaves thought or felt,' especially in the case of Greece – no matter how much we mine our evidence, or try by analogy with antebellum slaves in the United States or slaves in the present, to invent a voice for the slaves of antiquity.

Comparative evidence helped to raise possibilities and show differences, not fill in the gaps (e.g. 207-8). Historians should be explicit about what their modern positions and perceptions bring to their understanding of the past (11):

> To the confidence of the positivist working toward a clear, unblemished account of the ancient past, I prefer the self-conscious, self-critical, self-reflexive mode of knowing ... every perspective is particular, internally troubled, marked by conscious or unconscious investments. One can never know or understand all the determinants of one's inquiry, never fully represent the object. There is no single, true, whole picture of the past.

More fruitful, she felt, might be (12):

a perspective informed by a historically self-conscious version of cultural studies ... acknowledging a political engagement, attempting to address societies as problematic, heterogeneous, contradictory cultural fields ...

Yet even duBois' work, despite her stunningly clear programmatic statements, shows the strength of the traditional narrative we have seen weave itself into the work of other historians. She may embrace doubt, but there appears to be something guiding her on occasion towards a specific *type* of narrative. This might partly be explained by her desire to highlight negative facets of slavery that some classicists have tried to censor. In addition she wanted to examine 'hegemonic' discourse: patterns of thought which buttressed the existing social structure and its inequalities. She devoted most of her attention to this essentially conservative system of thought. This, however, can lead to giving less emphasis than deserved to other kinds of ideas (30):

If there are sometimes ... questions raised about the natural difference between master and slave, as in works of art, in certain moments of Aristophanic comedy or Euripidean drama, these questions are affirmed, answered, silenced, or drowned out by other sorts of acts ....

What has happened to a commitment to showing society to be a 'problematic, heterogeneous, contradictory cultural field'? There are times, indeed, when an under-problematised orthodox Anglophone view of slavery may be writing itself into her text. This is most notable in her treatment of drama.

Some fifth-century Athenian tragic plays appear to show some sympathy for slaves, particularly the aristocratic female war captives found in plays about the legendary Trojan War (e.g. Euripides' *Hecuba* and *Andromache*). The captives are given major roles and the meanness of their conquerors is laid bare. duBois suggested, however, that their status as (mythic) noble prisoners of war would have 'set them apart' from the slaves the audience bought and sold and lived with. The plays were not an attempt to explore the lives of, or create sympathy for, real slaves. Instead the slaves of drama allowed male citizens to probe their own 'anxiety' about falling into slavery by 'displacing it onto characters remote from them in time, in their class situation, and in gender' (133). Characters such as the vengeful enslaved queen Hecuba, for example, exhibited 'resources of pride and violence that the socially dead slaves of the classical city seem incapable of mustering' (ibid.). duBois followed Laura McClure in suggesting that the enslaved women may also have represented 'the political allegory of enslavement of the city itself' and the decline of traditional aristocratic power (141).

One can see the strength and subtlety of these arguments. There is an issue, however, with the consistency with which they are applied. It is easy to argue for a metaphorical reading of the 'aristocratic' prisoner-slaves, but what of the ordinary domestic slaves in drama? duBois says little about them, and the little she does say might suggest a desire, once again, to tell a particular type of story. There is little in duBois of the positive images of ordinary servants, for example in

Euripides' plays *Medea* and *Alcestis*, where slaves can show more common decency that some of the free. This may, admittedly, principally serve to emphasise the lack of virtue of free characters such as Medea and Heracles rather than any 'nobility' on the side of the slaves. duBois' decision not to give such slaves much attention is, nevertheless, still interesting. She did discuss the characterisation of nurses, a group of slaves who could develop close bonds with their masters and mistresses. She chose, however, to focus only on Phaedra's nurse in the *Hippolytus* who advised her mistress both cynically and badly (duBois 2003: 144-5, symbolic of the 'voice of low pragmatism and opportunism'). The more noble nurse in the *Medea* is mentioned by duBois only to make the point that slaves born in the house seldom spoke. This is one of a number of occasions where duBois *was* prepared to connect stage slaves with 'real' slaves (142-3). In Sophocles' *Women of Trachis* disaster falls on the household of Heracles after he brings the enslaved daughter of an enemy into his bed. duBois comments (143):

> The mention of the marital bed evokes the domestic life of the contemporary audience, and the sexual availability and threat represented by slaves in the house.

Later duBois discusses the 'animalisation' of the Trojan queen Hecuba. She becomes a slave and is then described with dog-like terms as she wreaks her revenge on her captors (147):

> Hecuba exemplifies a latent tendency among this dangerously unstable element of the human community,

.... Just so, the slaves of the city, ubiquitous and obedient to the commands of the masters in the audience, like faithful and obedient dogs, threaten the bodily security and integrity of the free.

Overall, potential evidence for sympathy towards slaves seems to be subjected by duBois to greater critical scrutiny than evidence for potential fear of them. *Anxieties* are real, sympathies apparently not. Again my point is not to suggest that duBois is necessarily wrong in any of this. Rather, I want to suggest that there are hidden assumptions in her interpretation.

In ch. 4 of her book duBois discussed 'The Slave Body', with a particular emphasis upon beating and torture, which she saw as reflecting the 'unruliness' of the slave. Like Johnstone, she argued that (102)

... it may even be possible to find, in the representations of slaves and slave bodies in antiquity, free persons' imagination of traces of resistance, of a refusal of complete objectification by slaves themselves.

She ended the chapter with a subsection entitled 'Murder' (111-12). We learn in a speech by the fifth-century Athenian orator Antiphon that a slave courtesan had been punished for poisoning her master (Antiphon 1.18-20). This is one of the very few surviving examples from classical Athens of slave violence against masters (see McKeown forthcoming (b)). The facts of the case were clearly disputed: the speaker claims that the slave believed she was giving her master a love-potion (allegedly provided by the speaker's evil step-mother). duBois concluded:

> We may discern here, leaking through a hegemonic account of the discipline, torture, and execution of the slave woman, traces of ingenious resistance, her choice for homicide and death over prostitution ...

While we *may* discern opposition to slavery and to prostitution here, there is actually nothing to suggest that we *should*: the speaker could, after all, be telling the truth about his step-mother. We just don't know. duBois continued (112):

> The slave body informs all the physical, spatial, sexual and social relations of ancient society, disturbingly persistent, potentially unruly, and ubiquitous.

It should be obvious that quite a lot depends on how we understand the word 'potentially', which can mean anything from common to uncommon. duBois began her next section (a conclusion for the whole chapter on the body of the slave) with a quotation from *The New Yorker* discussing modern US slaves who had burned 'their masters' beds'. She continued (112):

> Americans' own fear or shame or rage about slavery, the repression of our own history, can lead to blind spots, to denial, to projection and transference onto ancient culture, to suturing in our accounts of ancient society, to lacunae and omissions and denial.

Quite right. But is that what she is doing herself here, even if she left her readers to join the dots themselves without doing so explicitly herself? How far do her preconceptions about slavery mean that *she* wants to believe in high levels of slave resistance in the ancient world?

It is unfair to highlight from duBois' book just the issues I have raised about the reading of the dramatic slave or the slave body: the passages discussed form a (relatively) small part of it. They do, however, illustrate how powerful the 'story' of slave 'oppositionism' is within Anglophone historiography as it inscribes itself in even the very finest modern work. Historians of Greek history, perhaps as a function of the sparser nature of their sources, seem readier to consider the implications and methodological difficulties of the gaps in their evidence than other slave specialists. That, however, has not stopped them from trying to fill those gaps in a manner reminiscent of historians of the Roman world.

Conclusions

It is said that no battle plan survives engagement with the enemy intact. Similarly no historical interpretation tends to survive engagement with students. This book was partly born of frustrations in trying to convince students of some of the current orthodoxies about ancient slavery. This proved unexpectedly difficult. The process of trying to understand why was something of a revelation. I have tried to explain this in the previous chapters by focussing on a few examples of the best modern research.

Imagine a student of 2007 taking a trip in a time machine and taking a course on ancient slavery in 1937. We saw in Chapter 1 that much of what they might hear, particularly the emphasis on the negative effects of the racial mixture of slave and free, might sound very odd indeed to them. Returning home they would find a very different stress in a modern course on ancient slavery, usually emphasising resistance among slaves. What our student might not recognise was the extent to which the 'racial' positions of 1937 were subsequently by-passed rather than rebutted. Further, they might not recognise that the evidence for the 2007 'orthodoxy' might be almost as questionable as that of 1937. Each generation seems to have produced interpretations that generally fitted their wider ethical and social beliefs. The nature of the evidence gave them room to do this.

Differences in the interpretation of ancient slavery are not just a product of different eras, however. Curiously geography seems to have had an impact too. While we should be wary of exaggerating the coherence of modern 'schools' of thought, we saw in Chapter 2 that the stress given to particular aspects of ancient slavery can be very different in, for example, Germany and France. Fridolf Kudlien recognised that slavery could produce both social tensions and cruelty, but preferred to focus on the more human aspects of slavery which he felt allowed it to survive for so long. Marguerite Garrido-Hory instead chose to focus more on the tensions. Without trying to argue which historian was 'right' and which was 'wrong', it became clear that both critically tested testimony that threatened their views far more than testimony that apparently supported them.

It is obvious that the evidence concerning ancient slavery which has been used by modern scholars can actually support diametrically opposed positions. We saw in Chapter 3 that the evidence used to support the Marxist theories of Elena Shtaerman and Mariana Trofimova could easily be used to support a very different picture. In Chapter 4 we examined some of the work of Keith Bradley, perhaps the most important English-speaking historian of Roman slavery. We saw that his political engagement and passion, and his use of comparative evidence, do not necessarily provide an escape from the difficulty of the indeterminacy of much of the evidence. Even his apparently 'hard' evidence from Roman law could be interpreted in a number of different ways.

Literary scholars have produced some of the most sophisticated readings of ancient slavery (Chapter 5). They have been readier than most historians to accept the 'equifinality' of the evidence, its ability to tell more than one story. Even they, however, have tended to accept with little debate the 'orthodox' narrative (emphasising slave resistance) which their own approaches actually implicitly do much to question. While demographic specialists have sought to bring a promising 'scientific' approach to ancient slavery (Chapter 6), their models can be very sensitive to their starting assumptions, assumptions often moulded by the same literary sources whose bias they would seek to liberate us from. Their acceptance and recognition of the limitations of the evidence may, nonetheless, provide a useful model for how the history of slavery might be written. Finally, we have seen that some recent scholars of Greek slavery have been keenly aware of the difficulties in producing a narrative of the life of the ancient slave (Chapter 7). Despite this, they still appeared to want to emphasise slave resistance with far greater confidence than the evidence actually allowed.

Opposition of ancient slaves to their slavery is a theme that has recurred often in the work of the modern historians we have examined. I have raised serious doubts about this interpretation. It is not that I feel the story of widespread opposition among slaves, and of consequent 'anxieties' afflicting slaveowners, is untrue. There is enough evidence to suggest that it *might* be true. One might even go so far as to express the hope that it *is* true. How far can we show, however, that it is more plausible than alternative 'stories' with focus much less upon resistance? As with the racialist interpretation of slavery popular in the US and Britain in the 1930s (discussed in Chapter 1), it is evidently a story the evidence *allows* us to produce, and it is a story that many scholars evidently *want* to believe.

Whatever the similarities or differences between their approaches, all the authors we have examined faced problems when moving from isolated evidence to larger generalisations. This, however, reflects not personal failings, but a profound truth about the nature of historical evidence and the tools with which we seek to understand the past and create a picture from it. One might disagree (for example) with the emphases of both Bradley *and* Kudlien, but the problem actually lies not with their individual methods or approach so much as with the whole notion of 'emphasis' itself, what determines it and what it signifies. Historians can end up trapped in historically constructed boxes where sometimes quite arbitrary elements in their picture can appear as 'common sense'.

It was Terry Pratchett who introduced the idea of 'narrativium', an element in his imaginary Discworld which forced people to play out roles in particular stories or plots. The Anglophone history of ancient slavery (to take just one example) apparently contains 'plot lines' (concerning slave resistance) that continually try to write themselves. The writing of those plot lines (as we saw in our discussion of Keith Bradley's work) is entirely morally justifiable. If we simply accept the silences in our sources, we will condemn ourselves to writing (so to speak) the history of the prison-camp guards rather than that of their victims. We must therefore use our imagination to see the other 'plot lines'. Those plot lines, however, represent only *possible* readings of the evidence we have. They may be true, but they *need* not be. We must be careful not to 'rescue' the voice of the ancient slave by making it a distorted version of our own.

While there may be an infinite number of questions we can ask of the past, there are not, I believe, an infinite number of plausible answers to those questions. I have tried to show, however, that there are often *several* plausible answers. I am not therefore claiming that professional historians are 'making up' or 'inventing' their histories of ancient slaveries, but they do sometimes seem over-confident about some of the bits that really matter to them. Too often we operate as if there were single answers. Authors need to be prepared to show their readers more of the doubts and gaps. And readers have to be prepared to accept that there will be such doubts and gaps and that they represent real difficulties, not 'bad' history. Those difficulties face anyone trying to reconstruct both the past and also the world around them. The doubt and complexity needs to be faced. Antiquity in general, and ancient slavery in particular, offers a fascinating test of how difficult (or easy?) it can be to produce narratives from the past. I hope, however, that my story of the history of ancient slavery has given my reader some pause for thought about the way we understand not just the ancient but also the modern world.

Bibliography of Works Cited

Ancient texts

Translations and texts of the ancient texts cited can be found listed under the ancient author's name in the Loeb Classical Library published by Harvard University Press, with the exception of:

Daley, L.W. (trans.) (1961) *Aesop Without Morals: The Famous Fables, and a Life of Aesop* (New York: T. Yoseloff).

Perry, B. 1952 *Aesopica* (Urbana: University of Illinois Press).

Watson, A. (trans.) (1985) *The Digest of Justinian* (Philadelphia: University of Pennsylvania Press).

White, R.J. (trans.) (1992) *Artemidorus: The Interpretation of Dreams. Translation and Commentary* (Park Ridge, New Jersey: Noyes Classical Studies).

Modern works

Alföldy G. (1972) 'Die Freilassung von Sklaven und die Struktur der Sklaverei in der römischen Kaiserzeit', *Rivista Storica dell'Antichità* 2: 97-129.

Bagnall, R. and Frier, B. (1994) *The Demography of Roman Egypt* (Cambridge: Cambridge University Press).

Balsdon, J.P.V.D. (1979) *Romans and Aliens* (London: Duckworth).

Barrow, R.H. (1928) *Slavery in the Roman Empire* (London: Methuen).

Bettini, M. (1991) *Verso un' antropologia dell' intreccio e altri studi su Plauto* (Urbino: Quattro Venti).

Boulvert, G. (1970) *Esclaves et affranchis impériaux sous le haut-empire romain: rôle politique et administratif* (Napoli: Jovene).

Bradley, K.R. (1978) 'The age and time of sale of female slaves', *Arethusa* 11: 243-52.

——— (1984) *Slaves and Masters in the Roman Empire* (Bruxelles: Latomus).

——— (1987) 'On the Roman slave supply and slave-breeding', in M.I. Finley (ed.) *Classical Slavery* (London: Frank Cass) 42-64; new edn (2003) 53-81.

——— (1989) *Slavery and Rebellion in the Roman World, 140 BC–70 BC* (London: Batsford).

——— (1994) *Slavery and Society at Rome* (Cambridge: Cambridge University Press).

——— (2000) 'Animalising the slave: the truth of fiction', *Journal of Roman Studies* 90: 110-25.

——— (2001) 'Imagining slavery: the limits of the plausible', *Journal of Roman Archaeology* 14: 473-7.

Braund, S.M. (trans.) (2004) *Juvenal and Persius* (Cambridge, Mass.: Harvard University Press).

Brunt, P. (1971) *Italian Manpower* (Oxford: Clarendon Press).

Coale, A., Demeny, D. and Vaughan, B. (1983) *Regional Model Life Tables and Stable Populations* (New York: Academic).

Chantraine, H. (1967) *Freigelassene und Sklaven im Dienst der römischen Kaiser* (Wiesbaden: Steiner).

Dill, S. (1904) *Roman Society from Nero to Marcus Aurelius* (London; New York: Macmillan).

duBois, P. (2003) *Slaves and Other Objects* (Chicago: University of Chicago Press).

Duff, A.M. (1928) *Freedmen in the Early Roman Empire* (Oxford: Clarendon Press).

Dumont, J.Chr. (1974) 'Guerre, paix et servitude dans les *Captifs*', *Latomus* 33: 505-22.

——— (1987) *Servus: Rome et l'esclavage sous la République* (Rome: École française de Rome).

Dunkin, P.S. (1946) *Post-Aristophanic Comedy: Studies in the Social Outlook of Middle and New Comedy at both Athens and Rome* (Urbana: University of Illinois Press).

Fay, B. and Pom, P. (eds) (1998) *History and Theory* (Oxford: Blackwell).

Finley, M.I. (1998) *Ancient Slavery, Modern Ideology* (Princeton, New Jersey: Markus Wiener).

Fitzgerald, W. (1989) 'Horace, pleasure, and the text', *Arethusa* 22.1: 81-104.

——— (2000) *Slavery and the Roman Literary Imagination* (Cambridge: Cambridge University Press).

Fox-Genovese, E. et al. (eds) (1999) *Reconstructing History* (London: Routledge).

Frank, T. (1916) 'Race mixture in the Roman empire', *American Historical Review* 21.4: 689-708.

Frier, B. (2000) 'Demography', in A.K. Bowman, P. Garnsey and D. Rathbone (eds) *The Cambridge Ancient History*, vol. XI (Cambridge: Cambridge University Press) 787-816.

Gamaulf, R. (2001) 'Zur Frage "Sklaverei und Humanität" anhand von Quellen des römischen Rechts' in H. Bellen and H. Heinen (eds) *Fünfzig Jahre Forschungen zur antiken Sklaverei an der mainzer Akademie 1950-2000* (Stuttgart: Steiner) 51-72.

Garnsey, P. (1975) 'Descendants of freedmen in local politics: some criteria', in B. Levick (ed.) *The Ancient Historian and His Materials: Essays in Honour of C.E. Stevens* (Farnborough: Gregg) 167-80.

—— (1981) 'Independent freedmen and the economy of Italy under the Principate', *Klio* 63: 359-71.

—— (1996) *Ideas of Slavery from Aristotle to Augustine* (Cambridge: Cambridge University Press).

Garrido-Hory, M. (1981) *Martial et l'esclavage* (Paris: Belles Lettres).

—— (1998) *Juvénal: esclaves et affranchis à Rome* (Besançon: Presses Universitaires Franc-Comtoises).

Genovese, E. (1974) *Roll, Jordan, Roll: The World the Slaves Made* (New York: Pantheon Books).

Giardina, A. and Schiavone, A. (1981a) *Società romana e produzione schiavistica [1]: L'Italia: insediamenti e forme economiche* (Roma-Bari: Laterza).

—— and —— (1981b) *Società e produzione schiavistica [2]: merci, mercati e scambi nel mediterraneo* (Roma-Bari: Laterza).

—— and —— (1981c) *Società romana e produzione schiavistica: [3]: modelli etici, diritto e trasformazioni sociali* (Roma-Bari: Laterza).

Gordon, M.L. (1931) 'The freedman's son in municipal life', *Journal of Roman Studies* 21: 65-77.

Griffin, M. (1976) *Seneca: A Philosopher in Politics* (Oxford: Clarendon Press).

Harris, W.V. (1980) 'Towards a study of the Roman slave trade', *Memoirs of the American Academy at Rome* 36: 117-40.

—— (1999) 'Demography, geography, and the sources of Roman slaves', *Journal of Roman Studies* 89: 62-75.

Highet, G. (1973) 'Libertino patre natus', *American Journal of Philology* 94: 268-81.

Hopkins, M.K. (1966) 'On the probable age structure of the Roman population', *Population Studies* 20.2: 245-64.
—— (1978) *Conquerors and Slaves* (Cambridge: Cambridge University Press).
—— (1993) 'Novel evidence for Roman slavery', *Past and Present* 138: 3-27.
Hunt, P. (1998) *Slaves, Warfare, Ideology in the Greek Historians* (Cambridge: Cambridge University Press).
Hunter, R.L. (1985) *The New Comedy of Greece and Rome* (Cambridge: Cambridge University Press).
Iggers, G.I. (2005) *Historiography in the Twentieth Century: From Scientific Objectivity to the Postmodern Challenge* (Middletown, Conn.: Wesleyan University Press).
Isaac, B. (2004) *The Invention of Racism in Classical Antiquity* (Princeton: Princeton University Press).
Jenkins, K. (1991) *Re-thinking History* (London: Routledge).
—— (1995) *On 'What is History?': From Carr and Elton to Rorty and White* (London: Routledge).
—— (1997) *The Postmodern History Reader* (London: Routledge).
Johnstone, S. (1998) 'Cracking the code of silence: Athenian legal oratory and the histories of slaves and women' in S.R. Joshel and S. Murnaghan (eds) *Women and Slaves in Greco-Roman Culture: Differential Equations* (London: Routledge) 221-36.
Jongman. W. (2003) 'Slaves and the growth of Rome' in G. Woolf and C. Edwards (eds) *Rome the Cosmopolis* (Cambridge: Cambridge University Press) 100-22.
Joshel, S.R. (1992) *Work, Identity and Legal Status at Rome* (Norman, Oklahoma: University of Oklahoma Press).
Klees, H. (1975) *Herren und Sklaven: Die Sklaverei im oikonomischen und politischen Schrifttum der Griechen in klassischer Zeit* (Wiesbaden: Steiner).
—— (1998) *Sklavenleben im klassischen Griechenland* (Stuttgart: Steiner).
Konstan, D. (1983) *Roman Comedy* (Ithaca; London: Cornell University Press).
Kudlien, F. (1991) *Sklaven-Mentalität im Spiegel antiker Wahrsagerei* (Stuttgart: Steiner).
Kyrtatas, D. (1987) *The Social Structure of the Early Christian Communities* (London: Verso).
—— (1995) 'Slavery as progress: pagan and Christian views of slavery as moral training', *International Sociology* 10: 219-34.

McCarthy, K. (1998) '*Servitium Amoris: Amor Servitii*' in S. Murnaghan and S. Joshel (eds) *Women and Slaves in Greco-Roman Culture: Differential Equations* (London: Routledge) 174-92.

————— (2000) *Slaves, Masters, and the Art of Authority in Plautine Comedy* (Princeton, N.J.; Oxford : Princeton University Press).

McKeown, N. (1999) 'Some thoughts on Marxism and ancient Greek history', *Helios* 26.2: 103-28.

————— (forthcoming (a)) 'The sound of John Henderson laughing: Pliny 3.14 and Roman slaveowners' fear of their slaves', in A. Serghidou (ed.) *Fear of Slavery, Fear of Enslavement in the Ancient Mediterranean* (Bescançon: Presses universitaires de Franche-Comté).

————— (forthcoming (b)) 'Resistance among chattel slaves in the Classical Greek world', in P.A. Cartledge and K.R. Bradley (eds) *The Cambridge World History of Slavery*, vol. 1 (Cambridge: Cambridge University Press).

Manning, C. (1989) 'Stoicism and slavery in the Roman empire', *Aufstieg und Niedergang der römischen Welt* 2.36.3: 1518-43.

Martin, R. (1971) *Recherches sur les agronomes latins et leurs conceptions économiques et sociales* (Paris: Les Belles Lettres).

Mazza, M. (1975) 'Prefazione' in E.M. Shtaerman and M.K. Trofimova, *La schiavitù nell'Italia imperiale: I-III secolo* (Roma: Editori Riuniti) vii-xxxv.

Meyer, E.A. (1990) 'Explaining the epigraphic habit in the Roman empire: the evidence of epitaphs', *Journal of Roman Studies* 80: 74-96.

Morley, N. (1999) *Writing Ancient History* (Ithaca: Cornell University Press).

Mouritsen, H. (2004) 'Freedmen and freeborn in the necropolis of imperial Ostia', *Zeitschrift für Papyrologie und Epigraphik* 150: 281-305.

————— (2005) 'Freedmen and decurions: epitaphs and social history in imperial Italy', *Journal of Roman Studies* 95: 38-63.

Muecke, F. (1993) *Horace Satires II* (Warminster: Aris & Phillips).

Oliensis, E. (1998) *Horace and the Rhetoric of Authority* (Cambridge: Cambridge University Press).

Parker, H. (1989) 'Crucially Funny or Tranio on the Couch: the *servus callidus* and jokes about torture', *Transactions of the American Philological Association* 119: 233-46.

Parkin, T.G. (1992) *Demography and Roman Society* (Baltimore: Johns Hopkins University Press).

Perry, B. (1952) *Aesopica* (Urbana: University of Illinois Press).

Phillips, U.B. (1929) *Life and Labor in the Old South* (Boston: Little, Brown).

Prachner, G. (1980) *Die Sklaven und Freigelassene im arretinischen Sigillatagewerbe* (Wiesbaden: Steiner).

Raditsa, L. (1980) 'Augustus' legislation concerning marriage, procreation, love affairs, and adultery', *Aufstieg und Niedergang der römischen Welt* 2.13: 278-339.

Raskolnikoff, M. (1975) *La recherche en Union Soviétique et l'histoire économique et sociale du monde hellénistique et romain* (Strasbourg: A.E.C.R.).

Roberts, G. (ed.) (2001) *The History and Narrative Reader* (London; Routledge).

Rostovtzeff, M. (1926) *Social and Economic History of the Roman Empire* (Oxford: Clarendon Press).

Ste. Croix, G.E.M. de (1975) 'Early Christian attitudes towards property and slavery', *Studies in Church History* 12: 1-38.

—— (1983) *The Class Struggle in the Ancient Greek World* (London: Duckworth).

Saller, R. (2001) 'The family and society', in J. Bodel (ed.) *Epigraphic Evidence: Ancient History from Inscriptions* (London: Routledge) 95-117.

Scheidel, W. (1997) 'Quantifying the sources of slaves in the early Roman empire', *Journal of Roman Studies* 87: 156-69.

—— (2005) 'Human mobility in Roman Italy II: the slave population', *Journal of Roman Studies* 95: 64-79.

Shtaerman, E.M. and Trofimova, M.K. (1975) *La schiavitù nell'Italia imperiale: I-III secolo* (Roma: Editori Riuniti).

Scott, J. (1985) *Weapons of the Weak: Everyday Forms of Peasant Resistance* (New Haven; London: Yale University Press).

—— (1990) *Domination and the Arts of Resistance: Hidden Transcripts* (New Haven; London: Yale University Press).

Segal, E. (1987) *Roman Laughter: The Comedy of Plautus* (Oxford: Oxford University Press).

Sherwin-White, A.N. (1967) *Racial Prejudice in Imperial Rome* (Cambridge: Cambridge University Press).

Spranger, P.P. (1984) *Historische Untersuchung zu den Sklavenfigur des Plautus und Terenz* (Wiesbaden: Steiner).

Stampp, K. (1956) *The Peculiar Institution: Slavery in the Ante-Bellum South* (New York: Alfred A. Knopf).

Taylor, L.R. (1961) 'Freedmen and freeborn in the epitaphs of imperial Rome', *American Journal of Philology* 82: 113-32.

Thalmann, W.G. (1996) 'Versions of slavery in the *Captivi* of Plautus', *Ramus* 25.2: 112-45.

Thompson, H. (1993) 'Iron age and Roman shackles', *Archaeological Journal* 150: 57-168.

Tosh, J. (ed.) (2000) *Historians on History* (Harlow: Longman).

Treggiari, S. (1969) *Roman Freedmen During the Late Republic* (Oxford: Clarendon Press).

Vernant, J.P. (1980) *Myth and Society in Ancient Greece* (Brighton: Harvester Press).

Vogt, J. (1974) *Ancient Slavery and the Ideal of Man* (Oxford: Blackwell).

Waldstein, W. (1986) *Operae libertorum: Untersuchungen zur Dienstpflicht freigelassener Sklaven* (Stuttgart: Steiner).

————— (2001) 'Zum Menschsein von Sklaven' in H. Bellen and H. Heinen (eds) *Fünfzig Jahre Forschungen zur antiken Sklaverei an der mainzer Akademie 1950-2000* (Stuttgart: Steiner) 31-49.

Wallace-Hadrill, A. (1994) *Houses and Society in Pompeii and Herculaneum* (Princeton: Princeton University Press).

Ward-Perkins, B. (2005) *The Fall of Rome: and the End of Civilization* (Oxford: Oxford University Press).

Watson, A. (trans.) (1985) *The Digest of Justinian* (Philadelphia: University of Pennsylvania Press).

Weaver, P.R.C. (1972) *Familia Caesaris* (Cambridge: Cambridge University Press).

Weiß, A. (2004) *Sklave der Stadt: Untersuchungen zur öffentlichen Sklaverei in den Städten des römischen Reiches* (Stuttgart: Steiner).

White, H. (1978) *Tropics of Discourse: Essays in Cultural Criticism* (Baltimore; London: Johns Hopkins University Press).

————— (1987) *The Content of the Form: Narrative Discourse and Historical Representation* (Baltimore; London: Johns Hopkins University Press).

Wiedemann, T. (1985) 'The regularity of manumission at Rome', *Classical Quarterly* 35: 162-75.

Williams, G. (1995) 'Libertino patre natus: true or false?' in S.J. Harrison (ed.) *Homage to Horace* (Oxford: Clarendon Press) 296-313.

Woolf, G. (1996) 'Monumental writing and the expansion of Roman society in the early empire', *Journal of Roman Studies* 86: 22-39.

Zanker, P. (1975) 'Grabreliefs römischer Freigelassener', *Jarhrbuch der deutschen archäologischen Instituts und archäologischen Anzeiger* 90: 267-315.

Index